Bick Publishing House's
AWARD WINNING NONFICTION AND FICTION
For Teens & Young Adults

3 ALA Notable Books • Christopher Award
3 New York Public Library Best Books for Teens
VOYA Honor Book •YALSA Nominated Quick Picks for Teens
4 *ForeWord Magazine* Best Book of the Year Awards
International Book of the Month Selection
Junior Literary Guild Selection

PUBLISHERS WEEKLY calls Carlson's *Girls Are Equal Too: The Teenage Girl's How-to-Survive Book*, "Spirited, chatty, polemical...A practical focus on psychological survival." ALA Notable Book.

SCHOOL LIBRARY JOURNAL says of her book *Talk: Teen Art of Communication*, "Explores philosophical and psychological aspects of communication, encourages young people." *The Teen Brain Book: Who and What Are You*, "Practical and scientifically-based guide to the teen brain." *In and Out of Your Mind: Teen Science*, "Thought-provoking guide into the mysteries of inner and outer space." New York Public Library Best Books for Teens.

THE NEW YORK TIMES BOOK REVIEW says of Carlson's YA Science Fiction novel *The Mountain of Truth*, "Anyone who writes a teenage novel that deals with a search for the Truth must have a great respect for the young...speaks to the secret restlessness in the adolescent thinker." ALA Notable Book.

KIRKUS REVIEWS YA novel *The Human Apes*, "Vastness of this solution to the human dilemma." ALA Notable Book.

PUBLISHERS WEEKLY says of *Where's Your Head? Psychology for Teenagers*, co-authored by Dale Carlson and Hannah Carlson, M. Ed., C.R.C. "Psychological survival skills...covers theories of human behavior, emotional development, mental illnesses and treatment." Christopher Award.

THE MIDWEST BOOK REVIEW says of *Who Said What: Philosophy for Teens*, "Evocative, thought-provoking compilation and very highly recommended reading for teens and young adults." VOYA H

SCHOOL LIBRARY JOURNAL says of *Sto* ch
good advice is contained in these pages. ks
for Teens.

D1532995

PRAISE FOR
Recent Bick Publishing House Titles

Addiction: The Brain Disease

"*Addiction: The Brain Disease* breaks down the stigma regarding the nature of addiction. The raw truth regarding the physical, social, emotional, and psychological aspects of addiction, as well as help and recovery, are presented medically and through personal stories. This book unlocks the door of hope to any suffering from the disease of addiction to substances and/or behaviors. Carlson covers every base from medical neuroscientific information to self-tests to solutions in recovery."

— Jason DeFrancesco, Young Adult Editor, Yale-New Haven Medic

Cosmic Calendar: From the Big Bang to Your Consciousness

"Overview of the origin of the universe...brain, body, genes, sex, consciousness and intelligence...Carlson makes readers comfortable with her probing tone...accurate and informative...good addition science collections, good choice teen readers."

— Dodie Ownes, *School Library Journal*, goodreads.com

Are You Human or What?

"Humans tend to view themselves as separate from the rest of the species and life on Earth, instead of connected. However, humans have the ability to reprogram their thinking. Humanity will be responsible for its own next psychological evolutionary step by the choices it makes. The book...focuses on the brain as it relates to teen issues such as loneliness, aggression, and sex."

— *School Library Journal*

"Carlson examines the new science of evolutionary psychology, explaining the psychology of early man as it relates to human action today. The objective is to show how we can evolve further into human creatures who actually take and give joy in our lives...Evolutionary aspects of the fear system, aggression and anger, evil, sex, lust and human bonding are discussed, as well as how aspects of each emotion might be changed to result in more humane behavior...The objective of the book, to make teens recognize the source of their emotions and that they can control and even change them, is admirable."

— *Voice of Youth Advocates* (*VOYA*)

ADDICTION
THE BRAIN DISEASE

BOOKS BY DALE CARLSON

Teen Fiction:

Baby Needs Shoes

Call Me Amanda

Charlie the Hero

The Human Apes

The Mountain of Truth

Triple Boy

Teen Nonfiction:

Are You Human or What?

Cosmic Calendar: From the Big Bang to Your Consciousness

Girls Are Equal Too: The Teenage Girl's How-to-Survive Book

In and Out of Your Mind: Teen Science, Human Bites

Stop the Pain: Teen Meditations

TALK: Teen Art of Communication

The Teen Brain Book: Who and What Are You?

Where's Your Head?: Psychology for Teenagers

Who Said What? Philosophy Quotes for Teens

Adult Nonfiction:

Confessions of a Brain-Impaired Writer

Stop the Pain: Adult Meditations

with HANNAH CARLSON

Living with Disabilities: 6-Volume

Basic Manuals for Friends of the Disabled

with IRENE RUTH

First Aid for Wildlife

Wildlife Care for Birds and Mammals:

7-Volume Basic Manuals Wildlife Rehabilitation

ADDICTION

THE BRAIN DISEASE

DALE CARLSON
HANNAH CARLSON, M.Ed., LPC

Pictures By **CAROL NICKLAUS**

BICK
PUBLISHING
HOUSE

Bick Publishing House   2010   Madison, CT

Edited by Director Editorial Ann Maurer
Science Editor Jason DeFrancesco, Yale-New Haven Medic
Book Design by Jennifer A. Payne, Words by Jen
Cover Design by Greg Sammons

www.bickpubhouse.com

Library of Congress Cataloging-in-Publication Data

Carlson, Dale.
Addiction : the brain disease / by Dale Carlson and Hannah Carlson.
    p. cm.
Includes bibliographical references and index.
ISBN 978-1-884158-35-3 (alk. paper)
1. Self-actualization (Psychology)--Juvenile literature. 2. Addicts--Juvenile literature.
I. Carlson, Hannah. II. Title.
BF637.S4C364 2010
158.1--dc22   ˙

                                    2010002288

AVAILABLE THROUGH:
- Distributor: BookMasters, Inc., AtlasBooks Distribution,
  Tel: (800) BookLog, Fax: (419) 281-6883
- Baker & Taylor Books
- Ingram Book Company
- Follett Library Resources, Tel: (800) 435-6170 Fax: (800) 852-5458
- Amazon.com

Or: Bick Publishing House
307 Neck Road
Madison, CT 06443
Tel: (203) 245-0073 Fax: (203) 245-5990

Printed by McNaughton & Gunn, Inc. USA

IN DEDICATION

To all addicts addicted
to anyone or anything.

And to all those who teach us to be
free from the prisons of ourselves.

ACKNOWLEDGMENTS

To Ann Maurer, for her steadfast editorial
guidance throughout the years.

To Carol Nicklaus, for her award-winning pictures.

To Greg Sammons, for his brilliant covers.

To Jen Payne, for her perfect taste in interior design.

To Jason DeFrancesco, our Young Adult Editor,
for his Yale pharmacology expertise.

And to the minds of Daniel Dennett, Stephen Jay Gould,
Steven Pinker, and above all, J. Krishnamurti.

CONTENTS

FOREWORD

"All those things you write about in this book on addiction point to the effort to stay asleep, or at least insensitive and not awake. Isn't it the essence of addiction to escape life, to be kept occupied and insensitive? Life pricks us, wakes us up. We call being awake a pain, so we sedate ourselves, and roll over and go to sleep again."

R. E. Mark Lee, Executive Director,
Krishnamurti Foundation America

L et no one tell you life is easy. Life is hard. It can hurt. But instead of being taught how to understand psychological pain, and through understanding why we suffer, end the suffering, we are taught instead to escape it.

The trouble with this is that our escapes often turn into addictions and these hurt worse than the original trouble.

I have never met anyone who wasn't addicted to something. There are those who are addicted to substances like alcohol or other drugs. There are those who are addicted to food or shopping, to television, to the thrills of gambling, promiscuous sex, violence, or other dangerous behaviors. Some are burdened with neurological disorders that cause obsessive-compulsive behaviors in order to ward off the anxieties and panics of our brains' reactions to life.

Even the least insane among us has inherited, through evolution, culture, our personal pasts, an addiction to survival. Unless we understand the carnivorous-aggressive fears of our species, our human culture, and our own pain, we'll go on killing ourselves and each other trying to escape our own brains.

In the end, it is far less painful to understand our thoughts and feelings, than to wreck ourselves and our human population with our addictive escapes.

Psychological suffering is dissolved by seeing through it, not by trying to escape it through addiction.

— Dale Carlson

SECTION ONE

Chapter One
ADDICTION

Addiction Is a Progressive Brain Disease
Stages of Addiction
Evolutionary Origins of Addiction

What Is an Addict?

An addict is someone with a brain disease.

The addict's disease, either inherited at birth or formed by habit, is based in flawed brain chemistry. This creates a physical, psychological, emotional dependence on a drug. The physical need is biochemical. The psychological, or mental, emotional need, is obsessive. The desperate need for the drug grows irresistible, whether that drug is alcohol, heroin, marijuana laced or unlaced, methamphetamine, or cocaine. Other brain chemistry disorders—

depression, bipolar disease, Attention Deficit Disorder (ADD), or Obsessive Compulsive Disorder (OCD)—can sometimes create a need for addictive substances, especially if they aren't treated.

People can create an addiction to increasing their brain's own pleasure chemicals by a particular behavioral activity. Gambling or falling in love, for instance, produces a rush or high. These behaviors can also trigger drug abuse.

In addicts, there is a biochemically irresistible, mentally obsessive need for alcohol or other drugs. This physical drug dependence—the word drug also includes alcohol—is manifested by an addict's increased tolerance of the effects of the drug. This means that more and more of the drug is required to produce the same effect. Biochemical dependence also manifests itself by the severe, often painful, withdrawal symptoms that occur when the chemical substance is unavailable or withdrawn.

The 'go' system runs wild, and once the first drug or drink is taken, an addict loses control over stopping.

A most important symptom of addiction is easy for an addict and others to observe. This is the loss of control. After the first drug or drink, the 'go' systems of the addict/alcoholic's brain's pleasure circuits override the 'stop now' systems of the judgment circuits. The 'go' system runs wild, and once the first drug or drink is taken, an addict loses control over stopping.

The terrible danger is that using drugs and alcohol repeatedly over time alters an addict's brain chemistry and function. What the addict's brain thinks it needs to keep from going crazy only makes it crazier.

What Is Addiction?

Addiction is dependency on a substance or behavior, a drink or a drug, a person or possession you think you'll die or go insane without. It is not the same thing as enjoying an occasional pleasure when you're in the mood. *The trouble with fooling around with alcohol, or other possibly addictive drugs, is that you cannot know ahead of time whether or not your own personal biochemistry will be caught in addiction.*

DOES ANYONE SOUND LIKE YOU OR SOMEONE YOU KNOW?

Jake, 15   Most of my friends use at least two drugs to get a better high. The two drugs that are always around, in school and out, are weed, laced or unlaced with other drugs, and alcohol. Marijuana and beer are the regular ones we use. We smoke and drink at the same time. I don't think any of my friends have messed with heroin yet, but you never know.

Alyssa, 16 Last year we pretty much stuck to just beer and marijuana, but this year at parties I've mixed in Ecstasy, my mother's Percocet, and cocaine. We try different combinations for different highs, vodka and LSD, or we add mushrooms to beer and weed. Most kids I know stay away from heroin or smoking crack, but lots use their parents' prescription drugs instead of street drugs. Diet pills and over-the-counter cough medicine, too.

Terry, 14   We learned in class that combining drugs makes each drug 3 or 4 times more powerful. So mixing drugs can turn you into an addict faster, even kill you. It's scary, but it's fun. You don't know what's going to happen to you. Like narcotics cause severe respiratory depression. I had one friend who ended up in the hospital because she stopped breathing. But you don't want to hang out by yourself, so you try what everyone else is trying.

Statistics show that heroin is addictive for nearly 100% of people who use, morphine for 70%, alcohol for 10%. But these days, whatever you drink or use is often laced with extra drugs. You don't know what you're getting anymore from dealers that could trigger an addiction.

Addiction is a mental, emotional, physical need. It's a craving, a compulsive behavior, or an obsessive idea you feel you can never escape. An addiction may start as an adventure in altering your moods, your states of mind, to increase your sense of well-being, for an adrenaline rush. Or addiction may begin as just an impulse, or for social acceptance, an experiment among friends.

But if your inherited, genetic biochemistry predisposes you toward addiction, you may have just taken the first step into hell.

Addiction Is a Progressive Disease

Addiction, like many other diseases, is a progressive illness. Addiction can never be cured, but, like some other diseases, it can be arrested. Unfortunately, willpower alone does not work. Since an important psychological aspect of the disease is to defend the user's need to use, the addict adds to the problem by an unwillingness to realistically face the facts of his or her addiction. This is called denial (a polite word for lying) about the amount and frequency of use. It is part of the disease of addiction.

STAGES IN ADDICTION/ALCOHOLISM

Brief Description of Addiction Progression

As in many other illnesses, there are stages in the disease of addiction.

1. Social and tensional relief usage may not yet be apparent, either to the user or others. A drink or drug just looks and feels like a way to relax or fit in.

2. Onset of need for increased amounts to get the same effect (tolerance development). User/drinker needs a bit more after a period of days or weeks or months, to get the same effect.

3. Memory lapses, even blackouts. Blackouts are an alcoholic/addict's specialty. It looks to others like the user is talking and behaving as if she or he was still conscious and present, but the user does not remember a thing. This memory lapse can range from 'what did I do?' to 'where did I leave the car, my girlfriend, my clothes?'

4. Drinking and using become secretive, not just social, as the need to maintain a certain level of the drug in the system increases in order to ward off withdrawal symptoms. This is the start of having a few hits before the party, of keeping a secret stash nearby, of hiding drugs and bottles.

5. Loss of control over the amount of drugs taken: the first drink or other drug removes any inhibitions about stopping at all.

6. Rationalization, or excuses and blame, is the user's way out of taking responsibility. It's always the situation, the problems at home, or at school, at work or socially. It's always somebody else's fault that the user needs more drugs. Often, this stage is the beginning of aggressive behavior.

7. The next stages are guilt, remorse, isolation from friends, dropping responsibilities of school, work, family, neglect of self and health, loss of ability to perform sexually.

8. Dropping out of the world, health deterioration, insanity, criminal activity, jail, death will surely follow, without intervention and treatment.

What an Addict Is Not

What an addict is not is just some bad kid headed down the wrong street of life on purpose. What an addict is not, is somebody's mother or father who just happens to neglect, abuse, or abandon the family. Nor is an addict someone who just thinks it would be fun to live in the gutter, haunt crack houses, and end up in jail, insane, or dead.

The tragedy of addiction begins as an ordinary human hunger for pleasure, an escape from fear and psychological pain, or even a relief from boredom, loneliness, anxiety—it can end, without treatment, only in unimaginable horror.

To be born with the predisposition toward the biochemical disease of brain and body we call addiction is fundamentally no different than being born with a predisposition toward cancer or heart disease. The behavior caused by addiction is often criminal and always heart breaking, devastating to family and friends. But, as with any disease, understanding it, treating it, and changing its behavior is the remedy, not hanging. *And, like any other disease, it is treatable.*

Addiction is a Disease of the Brain

In *The Principles of Addiction Medicine from the American Society of Addiction Medicine (ASAM)*, addiction is described as a chronic relapsing brain disease. The American Psychiatric Association (APA) describes addiction as a disease of the brain, a chronic illness that needs ongoing care. Drugs wreck the brain's ancient reward circuits, and their interactivity with the brain's judgment circuits. The pleasure circuits are hijacked due to the increased spurts of the pleasure chemical dopamine produced in the brain by repeated

drug use. The neurochemical production of serotonin and norepinephrine is also affected.

The brain eventually stops producing its own pleasure chemicals, and without dopamine, serotonin, and norepinephrine, the
addict ends up by being groggy, depressed, unable to feel good.
Without increased use of the drugs they are hooked on, addicts are
then left with only depression and anxiety. These symptoms are
especially severe, since the APA has discovered that about 40% of
addicts suffer from co-occurring mental disorders such as bipolar
disease, clinical depression, anxiety disorder. And these are better
treated with prescribed antidepressants, SSRI medications such as
Prozac, Paxil, Lexapro, or SNRI medications such as Effexor under
psychiatric supervision.

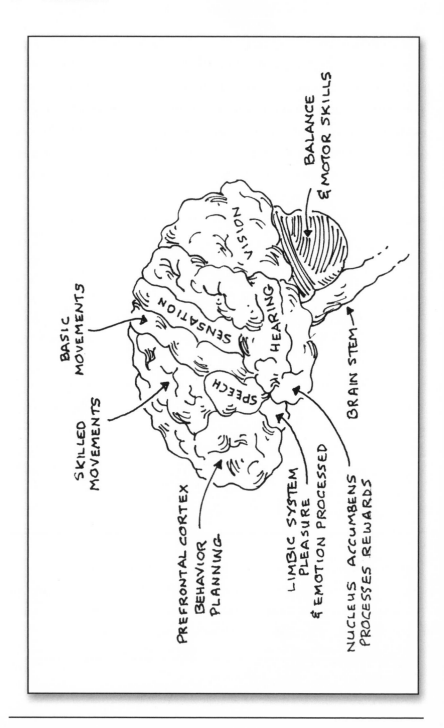

The Dead-End

But the horror of drug use is that the drugs stop working eventually, or addicts mainline and contract illness, or overdose and die. The point is, untreated addiction is a dead-end street. Worse than death perhaps is that certain drugs (see the Drug table in the dictionary section of this book) can create disorder in other parts of the brain permanently. Memory, coordination, judgment, balance are among the brain circuitries that may never recover from alcohol and other drug abuse. You may not die, but living is hell.

The Origins, the Evolution, of Addiction

Addiction is not a superficial problem about using too much and then getting some help. Addiction is not based on a few bad habits picked up in childhood or the teens for which the answer is a quick fix in a few meetings or a rehab.

Addiction has its origins deep in our human ancestry. Addiction has origins in our survival-behavioral-cultural heritage. And not just in our early human brains, but deep in our dinosaur brain where breathing and balance are regulated, in our animal midbrain, in our memory-processing hippocampus, in our amygdala, the seat of our emotions. Addiction has its origins in our very genes, the DNA of our genetic code.

Our Own Survival Genes Are the Origin of Addiction

Every cell in our bodies contains our DNA, the complete book of instructions on how to make that body and keep it alive to reproduce the genes. Through our DNA, our genes dictate for their own selfish need to survive, that we, as the gene's survival machines, also survive.

"EAT!" is the major instruction. "EAT, so you can stay alive and reproduce us, your genes!"

Of course, way back when, there was never enough to eat. It was hard work getting food. So the genes built in a reward system, pleasure chemicals that get released when our behavior keeps us alive and reproduces our genes.

Addiction is, therefore, actually rooted in the fallout from the physiological need to eat in order to live. Eating then forms a habit that transforms a physical need into a psychological demand for pleasure—a demand never satisfied, a constant, an ever unsatisfiable demand as the need to eat to live is basically unending. *This unending feeling of need is permanently embedded in the human brain.*

To repeat: to make sure we meet survival needs, like feeding and reproducing, our bodies, our genes give us a chemical reward system.

The Rewards of the Brain's Own Drugs

When humans eat or have sex, all kinds of chemicals are released in brain and body that give us pleasure and a temporary freedom from anxiety over the problems and dangers of living. There is just nothing like sex and the chemicals sex releases, to take your mind off of your self and your problems. Eating, especially foods high in sugar and fat, also releases rewarding chemicals and therefore good feelings into the whole body. And both sex and eating bring other rewards for these survival activities—orgasm, a full belly, affection, acceptance, position, safety in the pack, and a momentary escape from harsh realities.

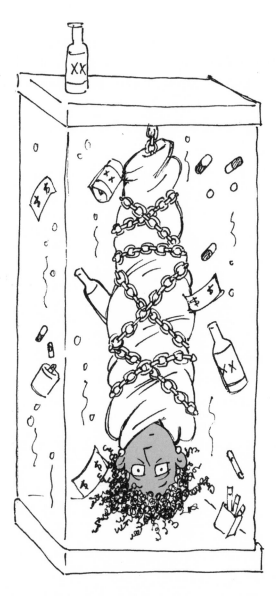

Addiction is a craving, a compulsive behavior or
an obsessive idea you feel you can never escape.

The Evolution of an Addict

What happens in the brain cells of someone with a predisposition toward addiction is genetic. Among the 3,000 million letters in the genes that affect the chemistry in our 100 trillion brain cells, those that determine the release of pleasure chemicals are faulty.

Although scientists have not determined all the genetic aspects of alcoholism and other drug addictions, many agree there are addiction genes. These genes are the ones that affect the pleasure-releasing chemicals in the brain like dopamine and serotonin. There have been experiments with altering such genes in laboratory animals, but the trouble with altering genes as a treatment for addiction is that genes affect more than one thing. Altering the dopamine-release gene, for instance, also affects risk-taking.

Altering the seratonin-release gene also affects the sex drive, as does altering the norepinephrine-release gene. Altering genes can have unintended consequences.

Snipping and Pasting Genes, or Culture and Environment?

There is also another problem. While we snip and paste our DNA to control our evolutionary characteristics, we cannot ignore the effects of our human environment. Among animals, human beings are uniquely dominated by cultural environment. This means that even if it is not inherited in the genes, people can turn themselves into addicts with drug habits that change the brain's chemistry. Even if we're not born with genes that predispose us toward addiction, we can turn ourselves into addicts by altering our own brains with the abuse of drugs.

The good news is that human beings also have another unique capacity. We are not only conscious, we are a self-conscious species. We can learn to understand. We can access the intelligence to understand that changing behavior can change human plastic brains faster even than evolution. Specifically, by changing our behavior, we can rewire, cause an actual mutation, in our own brains.

As evolutionary Darwinian scientist Richard Dawkins says in his book *The Selfish Gene*, we must understand what our genes are up to, because then we have a chance to upset their designs—something no other species can do. And, as anthropologist Stephen Jay Gould always adds, "Biology is not destiny."

We are not condemned to addiction by our genes.

But only if we take the trouble to understand ourselves, evolutionarily, biologically, psychologically.

An Addict's Evolutionary Problem

Natural selection for survival favors genes that control their gene machines (us)—to make it! Active addicts won't make it. There is something wrong with the genes, a loss of control over the production of pleasure chemicals, a loss of control over how much is enough. The pleasure chemistry isn't working right—there is never a lasting satisfaction, and more is always required—more of whatever is being used, drunk, swallowed, inhaled, huffed, snorted, injected, more of any pleasure chemical. There is no off button; the brain chemistry reward system isn't regulated properly. Not everyone is a perfect specimen of the species, but twisted chemistry can be fought as well as any other physical battle. By changing our

This unending feeling of need is permanently embedded in the human brain.

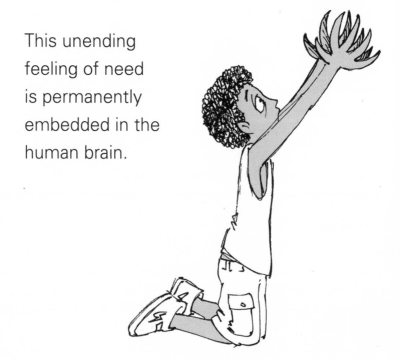

behavior, we can mutate our brains and control our own evolution. We do not have to let Nature, with its genes, eating and sexual behaviors, environmental and climactic conditions, be the only factor involved in human evolution.

To Be Human and Alive
Is to Be Uncomfortable

The deal is, if you only look at the way you feel, to be human and alive is to be uncomfortable. Unlike the brains of other animals, human animal brains don't just fear what is in front of us. We have evolutionarily developed predictive imaginations to help keep us alive and safe from danger in order to make up for our lack of relative strength and speed. This means we can not only use our imaginations to predict future dangers, we actually live in constant fear of those dangers and what might happen to us. We are both cursed and blessed with thought and imagination.

Joy happens, but not predictably, and not in the absence of intelligent, orderly, loving behavior. This last being difficult, and thought always full of fear of the future, we find escape from our frightened thoughts through entertainment, from politics and religions to stories, movies, TV games, competitive sports, and the mood-altering chemicals of drugs or repetitive behaviors.

Why Bother to Quit?

Why bother to endure the agony—and it can be physical and psychological agony—of withdrawal, of going through treatment and the often-long process of recovery?

You cannot really scare an addict, not with death, anyway. Many addicts/alcoholics will tell you they would just as soon be dead.

As for mental suffering, addicts already know about that, or they wouldn't be self-medicating to begin with.

The initial reasons to quit, to kick, to stop drinking and using, differ for each addict. But to stay stopped is a whole other thing, which we will talk about at the end of Chapter Four. It is the evolutionary imperative of self-interest that has crippled humans psychologically. And it is this we must examine in order to be free from the psychological suffering at the bottom of addiction.

Addiction, whether to drugs or obsessive behaviors, brings predictable comfort, moments of escape, freedom from anxiety, even the intense pleasure of being temporarily high.

But there is a price for selling yourself out for the quick relief of a buzz. Not just jail, insanity, or death through drinking alcohol or using other drugs. Not just mental and psychological despair through addictive thought, ideology, and behavior.

The price of addiction is never to have really lived your life at all. The price is oblivion.

The price of addiction is never to have really lived your life at all. The price is oblivion.

STORY They Called Me Bear

grew up in a project. I got beaten up a lot. My best friend's family was black, mine was white, and we both got beaten up not only because we hung out together but because we flaunted our friendship. My other friends stayed inside and out of trouble. I stayed outside with my friend. I was eight years old.

There was a safety zone near the project, a park where we played ball, protected by the crowds of people. The excitement, the high, was in getting to the safety zone, even knowing that a bunch of guys might beat me up again on the way. My heart was in my throat, but the excitement of getting to the park outweighed the fear and the pain.

The smart thing would have been to stay in the house — but my addiction to the excitement of risk behavior had begun.

Until I was fifteen, looking for fights was my major excitement. Then, when I got a job at a roller-skating rink, I learned the thrill of planning to rob the place. And the devious thrill of stealing had begun — cars, bikes, and the beginning of dealing drugs dishonestly. I learned fast how to charge more and pay less for my supply — a new thrill — getting away with something, playing the sides against the middle. Going from selling pot to selling cocaine brought me into the gangs from senior year on.

We moved up to motorcycle clubs in our late teens. I was now officially entering the life of crime. There was not only the exciting threat of being caught, but the high of the life-risking speed of the bike itself. Being associated with a motorcycle club meant certain other behaviors: orders might be given to beat up members of other clubs, to sell guns as well as drugs, and behave as ruthlessly as possible to keep up respect. Big patches, a set of rags, the club colors had to be worn, always a weapon carried—always you were a walking target. I risked even more danger and disobeyed the rules about going out alone. I went to other clubs' bars by myself, got beat up and thrown into alleys where my club had to pick me up in a shoot-out. My violent and risky behavior stood out even in a motorcycle club: they called me Bear.

The next level of danger after the motorcycle club stage was the life of full-blown drug addiction: living on the streets; going into drug dens, crack houses, dangerous in themselves because people were glad to kill you real quick. Walking with a pocketful of money through gang neighborhoods looking to cop drugs was risky behavior all by itself. And when I had no money, it was even more dangerous to steal a car, stop near one of the fifty guys holding out drugs to sell, and grab the money, the drugs, or both. The high was almost as much in getting the drugs as the drug itself.

Risk behavior was my whole life. Friendships and relationships were transient. I would destroy them with my risk behavior.

Toward the end, the excitement of the adventure had to be increased, going to New York City instead of small town downtown, going from smoking a neighborhood joint to stealing a city kilo.

Consequences interrupted my risk behavior when I ended up in jail, but only until I got out. I finally got arrested for selling guns—the RICO act put whole gangs in jail for dealing automatic weapons—and I hit my bottom.

Jail, the threat of death, and certainly drug insanity were the end of what had once been exciting. I wasn't even getting high anymore from any of it, so what was the point.

Risk behavior that started out as fun and exciting ended in nothing but physical and mental pain.

It was time for recovery. In my case, I had to face down a couple of relapses, but my program works now, my friendships last, my love for a woman grows deeper with my commitment to recovery.

Note: Bear's addiction to risk is like the addiction to romance, not a death wish but a high.

Chapter Two

ADDICTION TO SUBSTANCES

Major Causes of Addiction:
Genes, Evolution, Environment, Yourself
Brain Chemistry
Tolerance, Withdrawal, Treatment, Recovery

Three Causes of Addiction:
Genes, Environment, and You

No one has to become an addict.

No one inhales for you, or injects you illegally, or pours a drink or a pill down your throat but you.

No one stands in the way of recovery and treatment but you, if addiction catches you or you catch addiction.

That said, check out your genes. Watch out for the minefield called environment.

Your Genes

Inherited genes can make you more vulnerable to the biochemical reactions your brain/body has to alcohol and other drugs. Just as some people and their families have inherited genetic tendencies toward diabetes, or allergies, some people have inherited tendencies, a predisposition, toward the genetic biochemistry of drug and alcohol addiction. Biogenetics can explain why some kids get hooked on drugs pretty quickly, and some not at all. It doesn't seem fair, but there it is.

BREAKING NEWS...It will not have escaped you, if you're paying attention, that there are more people on Earth than ever before. Wild animals control their populations by dying young. They almost never die of old age. Humankind, however, bears too many children who live too long. Sickness, war, and starvation have traditionally kept populations in check. Now, drug abuse, with its increasingly international terrorist battles, national and local gang murders, but primarily the vast numbers of teen drug deaths is becoming an equal-opportunity check on human overpopulation.

It's bad enough humanity kills its young in wars. Don't help out by killing yourselves.

- -

No one has to become an addict. No one inhales for you, or injects you illegally, or pours a drink or a pill down your throat but you.

- -

Check Out Your Family

1. Check out your family tree for previous addicts and alcoholics. Did your grandparents drink daily, do your parents drink daily? Did any of them rely heavily on pills? Use illegal party drugs?

2. Ask your parents, grandparents, aunts, uncles, cousins, even close family friends for information, stories, rumors about any and all addictive behaviors and misbehaviors, as one kind of addiction often leads to another. This information has to do with family biochemistry that could affect you, not family values and morals or gossip.

It has to do with family biochemistry that could affect you, not family values and morals or gossip.

3. If the words 'addict' or 'alcoholic' are too strong for your family members, ask about any 'cravings' or 'habits' or 'wild' behavior. Eating too many sweets could indicate diabetes, and diabetes is biochemically first cousin to alcoholism. Both are an addiction to, and an inability to properly metabolize sugar molecules found in sweets and carbs as well as booze. Taking too many risks, gambling too much, might indicate an addiction to the adrenaline rush or the dopamine spurt in one's own brain. Keep in mind that cravings, desires, are part of our evolutionary chemistry. Since we are wired to chase food and sex, enjoy the excitement of rewards, we just need to know if members of our families let any of this natural behavior turn into an addiction, get out of control.

4. Ask also about any family mental illness such as schizophrenia or bipolar disorder, mood and personality disorders—depression, mood swings, severe anxiety, obsessive compulsive behavior, from gambling to rat-packing, hoarding. The negative effects from these moods and behaviors can become triggers for self-medicating and drug abuse.

But always know, no matter what you find out, biology is not destiny! Behavioral heredity is not destiny!

Treatment and help are always available to change your behavior and rewire your brain circuits!

The human brain is plastic, capable of change!

You may have come from a family with a propensity for abusing mind-altering substances. But as Bill Wilson, founder of Alcoholics Anonymous, and many experts in alcohol and drug abuse on our reading list at the back of this book have agreed—it takes more than genes to make an addict an addict.

Our Ancestors Used Drugs

Our ancestors were chewing coca leaves to alleviate pain and to get high, thousands of years before modern chemistry made crack cocaine available.

Our forebears cured and smoked marijuana, used mushrooms for medicinal purposes, or to achieve religious ecstatic states, even just for a buzz to make hard lives bearable, for all we know.

They used the poppy to make opiates, one of the oldest forms of medical analgesic, or mental escape.

Humans have been drinking alcohol ever since there was fruit dropping from trees and fermenting enough to produce a rush.

Primate watchers report that any gorilla, any chimpanzee, orangutan, or gibbon knows which forest leaves medicinally help relieve a tummy-ache.

Not all of them became addicts. But those among us who are addicts have inherited our predispositions towards our disorders through our genes going back hundreds of thousands, even millions, of years.

Your personal likelihood of becoming an alcoholic or drug addict, your propensity toward depression or an anxiety or behavioral or emotional disorder that could trigger self-medication and

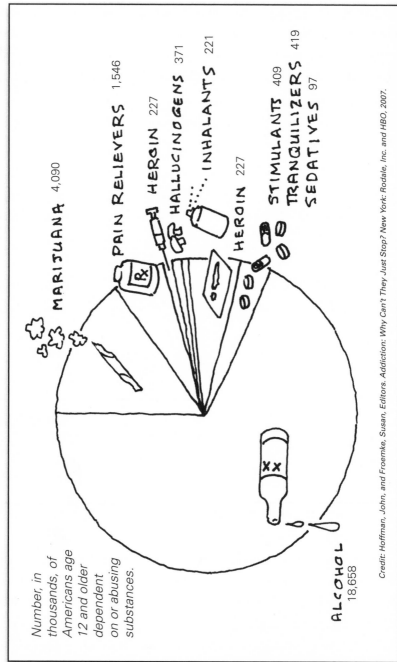

THE SUBSTANCES OF ABUSE

Number, in thousands, of Americans age 12 and older dependent on or abusing substances.

MARIJUANA 4,090

PAIN RELIEVERS 1,546

HEROIN 227

HALLUCINOGENS 371

INHALANTS 221

HEROIN 227

STIMULANTS 409

TRANQUILIZERS 419

SEDATIVES 97

ALCOHOL 18,658

Credit: Hoffman, John, and Froemke, Susan, Editors. Addiction: Why Can't They Just Stop? New York: Rodale, Inc. and HBO, 2007.

addiction, may well be genetically determined. But we all inherit predispositions toward diseases and disorders through our genes from parents, grandparents, and our more ancient forebears. And it still takes more than genes to make an addict an addict.

Increased Risk in Parent Addiction

In *Teens under the Influence: The Truth about Kids, Alcohol, and Other Drugs—How to Recognize the Problem and What to Do about It* by Katherine Ketcham and Nicholas A. Pace, M.D., the authors report test findings. "If one parent is alcoholic, the risk of addiction for the child is 40 percent, or about 4 times the risk of the general population. If both parents are alcoholics, the risk increases to about 60 percent." About half of all Americans age twelve or over are drinkers, the authors report. Basic facts for alcohol dependence also hold true for addictions to other drugs. Marijuana, cocaine, heroin, methamphetamines, party drugs, over-the-counter and prescription drugs—no matter what the drug, the same biochemical factors underlie all potentially addictive drugs.

The genes involved in addiction are many and complicated (it isn't a single gene), and, of course, interact with other genes for emotional and mental and behavioral disorders.

The Human Brain: Is It Helping
Us Survive, or Trying to Kill Us?

Research has shown that all drugs of abuse activate the brain's pleasure pathway. Food, exercise, lovemaking, music, and whatever else turns you on activate a surge in the level of the brain's neurotransmitter dopamine. The experience is then "logged into the brain's limbic system, which, in addition to being the center for pleasure

and emotion, houses key memory and motivation circuits. This is what the brain's dopamine pathway does; it records both the actual experience of pleasure and ensures that the behaviors that led to it are remembered and repeated," say the editors John Hoffman and Susan Froemke of *Addiction: Why Can't They Just Stop?* based on an HBO documentary on drug abuse.

Our Brain Chemistry's Pleasure Cravings

Remember that the whole dopamine system evolved from the evolutionary biological imperative of survival. Food meant survival, sex meant survival, and going back for more of both meant survival of whatever species you belonged to.

The first time we take alcohol or drugs—including caffeine and nicotine as well as party or club drugs, over-the-counter or prescription drugs—dopamine levels spike higher than they do with food or even sex and that experience is remembered. It is stored in the brain's hippocampus (memory) and amygdala (emotion). The spiked pleasure levels will recede, but they are recorded in the brain's memory.

The next time we use, the spike is lower, the crash is deeper. After repeated drug use, the brain no longer produces its own dopamine. It craves more and more of the addicted substance, fooled into thinking the drug is necessary for comfort and even functional survival.

Without the drug, depression follows, along with uncomfortable, even painful physical symptoms. If we use external opiates and opioids, the brain may stop making internal endorphins altogether. Without endorphins, the body cannot regulate discomfort or pain, cannot make itself comfortable or pain-free. Obviously, what we can no longer produce ourselves, we have to keep taking in.

Drug withdrawal and craving may also become a permanent cycle, and recovery may include understanding that these symptoms have now become a permanent problem that has to be dealt with for the rest of the addict's life. Brain damage, damage to the nerve circuits in the brain from hard drugs derived from coca leaves and the poppy may also be permanent.

The brain craves more and more of the addicted substance, fooled into thinking the drug is necessary for comfort and even functional survival.

This is vastly oversimplified. But understanding even just this bit of neurobiology shows us that it is the last drug taken, the last drink or cigarette that causes the craving for the next one—and the only way to halt the craving, is to stop taking the drug. Don't confuse the feeling of craving with the facts. You do not actually need the drug: you can just wait out the craving until it passes—and it will pass. If you haven't gone too far with your drug addiction, your brain will again start producing its own real, pleasurable dopamine. That is, once you stop feeding it the fake stuff.

- -

If you can't stop on your own, ask for help.

1. Talk to people you can trust to help you stop.

2. Telephone. Use the phone numbers at the back of this book. There are fellow alcoholics and addicts who answer phones and will understand and direct you to the meetings near you to meet teens who have been through the same thing. They will understand and help you.

- -

While addiction is addiction and the symptoms are
generally similar, each addict is different.

Environment

The genes for addiction also interact with young people's environment. Genes alone won't get you drunk or high. You can either
irritate your inherited genes by using your environment as an ex-
cuse to drink and use to ruin your life—or you can understand
these factors and escape or treat your addiction.

Environment Triggers the Genes

We use and abuse alcohol and drugs, we escape into addictive behaviors like compulsive sex and gambling, for a lot of personal and
environmental as well as inherited reasons.

As senior research psychologists state in *Addictions: Why Can't
They Just Stop?* "The origins of addictions are as varied as the addicts themselves. Each case needs to be understood as a human
faced with a particular set of variables—parents, economic status,

psychological environment—all of which are relevant but no single one of which can rightly be called decisive."

- This is why treatment and recovery have to be specific to each addict.

- This is why treatment and recovery are never as simple as "just saying no".

- MRIs of the brain, and other body organs such as liver and kidney, blood and urine tests and other medical diagnostic procedures can help establish the various physical

The beginnings of addictions are as varied as the addicts themselves.

conditions and stages of addiction, the curve of tolerance from low to high to low again, the type and severity of withdrawal symptoms.

• And not only is each person's addiction based on different factors, but since addiction is a progressive mental and physical and emotional disease, it is necessary to understand what stage each person's addiction has reached and identify the symptoms at each stage of progression, such as

a) How much time is spent using or acting out the behaviors?

b) Is the drug or behavior interfering with ordinary daily activities like school, work, and relationships?

c) How much lying, stealing, avoidance is going on?

d) What kinds of physical symptoms are evident?

The point is, while addiction is addiction and the symptoms are generally similar, each addict is different. Personal problems and stories vary from person to person. These factors must be understood by the addict and friends and family, and the treatment/recovery support team. People are people: they are not just cardiac cases or cancer survivors or alcoholics or addicts.

ENVIRONMENTAL TRIGGERS

Some Important Environmental Triggers

1. Teenagers may have spent their childhood surrounded by adults who consistently used and abused substances and escapist behaviors like too much entertainment, gambling, sex, to relieve their stress. Teens simply learned from the adults around them that escape rather than understanding and communication was the way to deal with fears, anxieties, and trouble.

2. Teens who have been molested or otherwise mistreated are more likely to abuse substances and behaviors. Post-traumatic stress and anxiety disorders, fears of all kinds leave them vulnerable to whatever relief they can find.

3. Inner environment as well as outer environment counts as a trigger. Teens who suffer deeply from loneliness and isolation, fears and anxiety, depression and insecurity, are more likely to drink and use.

4. Many teens remain undiagnosed for serious mental illness such as bipolar or depressive disorders, and behavioral or attention disorders such as ADHD or oppositional defiance, uncontrolled rage.

5. Teens who are bullied because of racism or gender (girls, gays, Lesbians, transgenders, transvestites, transsexuals); for size (too big, too small, too fat or too thin); teens who are victimized by poverty, or by ethnic background; those who are made fun of for a physical defect, or for any other personal differences are more likely to abuse drugs or become addicts, alcoholics.

6. Teens and pre-teens may start using drugs and alcohol to ease stress at home or at school, just to feel more comfortable in their own skins, feel happier, or at least less unhappy, less angry or lonely or scared. They may use or drink just to fit in with other kids, or because they admire kids who do use, or even just because they're tired of the feeling of being left out when they say 'no'. They may at some point just be attracted to the risks involved, the danger of drug life and living on the edge.

The reasons are endless: the risk everywhere. And you don't have to be abused, or have a genetic predisposition or a bad environment. Just by using drugs, you can turn yourself into an addict. Anyone can become an addict, any time.

EXPERIMENT:
Stress Test Yourself

We all try to escape the stress of everyday life: school, jobs, parents, friends, ourselves with all our fears, anxieties, the whips, self-criticism, and put-downs of our internal voices.

What do you do to escape from yourself and your life? Ask yourself: how much time do I spend zoning out?

1. **Electronically:**
    -   Internet: Facebook, MySpace, Twitter, etc., movie sites, sex sites, games, shopping, random surfing, IMing friends
    -   texting, telephoning, using your cell's app's
    -   TV
    -   Ipod
    -   video games
    -   you fill in what else and count the time

2. **Using substances to change or lift mood, relieve stress, anxiety, loneliness**
    -   junk food, chocolate, carbs, soda, energy drinks
    -   alcohol
    -   cigarettes
    -   drugs

3. **Using excessive behavior to change or lift mood, relieve stress**
    -   sleep
    -   sex, romance
    -   gambling, risk-taking
    -   gossiping, bullying
    -   over-exercising, overeating
    -   shopping

What we want, the aim of all of the above activities is to increase the flow of the pleasure chemical dopamine in our brains to override any bad feelings. The whole dopamine system, remember, evolved from the evolutionary, biological imperative to survive. Eating food meant survival. Sex meant survival. The more we did of both, the more we ensured the survival of the whole species, and the more our brains rewarded us by releasing pleasure chemicals.

But we have gotten greedier than our ancestors. We want more pleasures than just food and sex. We want more pleasures more often. But the downside of too much pleasure, too often, are tolerance and withdrawal, the two most telling and devastating aspects of addiction.

It's really amazing what
humans are willing to
risk for a high.

Tolerance and Withdrawal

TOLERANCE: the need for more and more of whatever you're on to get the same effect.

WITHDRAWAL: the symptoms manifested when whatever you're on is stopped: cravings, shakes, nausea, sleep problems, increased aggression, anger, irritability, restlessness, crying or laughing jags, mood swings, decreased appetite, cramps, muscle aches, headaches, memory lapses, chronic fatigue, sullen behavior, social isolation, rule-breaking, risk-taking. More severe withdrawal symptoms can include stroke, stopped breath, heart attack, and brain damage. (It's really amazing, when you think about it, what humans are willing to risk for a high.)

Horrors of Addiction

Among the horrors of addiction in teens is that the addiction itself is such a shock. One shock is that you can get hooked the first time you use, even if you don't have addiction genes. Another shock is that addiction among the nicest and the smartest, the environmentally safest of teens can lead to violence, crime, jail, and death. If the addiction is to inhalants, but most particularly to hard drugs derived from coca leaves and the poppy, especially crack and heroin (much of which contains chemical fillers mixed into street drugs by dealers to increase the high), brain damage, and damage to the nerve circuits in the brain, may be permanent.

Obviously, eating food, going shopping, falling in love, enjoying the endorphins released by exercise, using your computer, listening to music are all part of daily life. Just as obviously, many of us, pre-teens, teens, and adults are going to experiment—try a cigarette, take a drink, gamble on something, experiment with sex—at some point in our lives.

It's when anything, any one, any activity, above all, any substance, turns into an obsessive idea that leads to a repetitive, compulsive use or behavior that addiction begins.

And one of the greatest shocks of all for an addict/alcoholic is the feeling of being unable to stop doing whatever you're addicted to.

Treatment and Recovery

For an alcoholic/addict, these two words can mean hell and heaven. It is perfectly true, the only cure for addiction is…

JUST STOP
Simple enough.

The trouble is, just stopping is often painful, usually terrifying, and always hard to do. Not sometimes, always.

1. You'll need to reach out to other people for help and support, whether that is to find and go to detox or a treatment center, or find and go to support group meetings like A.A. or N.A. Asking for help is difficult and emotionally painful for alcoholics/addicts to do, what with anger at others and oneself, pride in living in lonely isolation for so long without help. There is also the damage done to other lives, parents and friends who may not have much faith, who are hurt and angry, and you'll need to learn how to deal with this, drug-free.

2. Psychological dependency on your once always-present friend the drug has become is hard to overcome.

3. Physical dependency that in withdrawal causes uncomfortable, sometimes painful symptoms is also hard to overcome.

4. The changes in behavior, attitude, ways of living and thinking required in order not to pick up again may be alien, difficult to learn, difficult to keep up day after day.

However: as hard as it can be to stop—to go on using is harder. Only more misery, loneliness, fear, madness, homelessness, sickness, jail, and death await you.

I know. Dale Carlson has been a recovering alcoholic/addict, clean and dry, for 32 years.

STORY Love Story

Lara and Joe were so much in love it made each of them crazy to be apart. Since they had fallen in love while they were in their sophomore year high school play together, they had never spent a day without touching or talking.

If family occasions or work or school separated them for more time than they could tolerate, Lara grew desperately anxious and depressed. Joe's reaction when he was separated from his girl was anger and a feeling of lonely isolation. They married right after graduation, even against their families' wishes. They were just eighteen.

Joe was good with electronics and found a job right away in their town's local repair shop. Lara discovered she was pregnant almost right away. Instead of getting a job, she spent her days drifting and dreaming and looking out the window, waiting for Joe to come home.

Joe was proud of the idea of being head of his own family, and moved them out of her parents' basement into a tiny apartment of their own. Joe worked long hours for not much money. Lara fixed up their two rooms and waited, dinner ready, for Joe to come home, often late, from a tiring day.

One evening, he found her waiting for him as her mother had waited for her father, with a tray on their small coffee table. She had squeezed a little extra from their housekeeping money, as her mother had, to lay out beer, glasses, pretzels. If they couldn't afford to go out with their friends, Lara said, at least they could have their own little after-work party in the evenings.

After a while, Joe noticed, there was a lot more beer on the coffee table than food on the dinner table, and extra six-packs stacked in the kitchen. But he didn't complain. The beer made them both feel better than food, anyhow. Joe felt like a king, with his pretty, pregnant, teenage wife, his clean home, and good job that paid enough to support his family.

Within a year, the scene had darkened.

Lara had discovered something about herself: she could not be alone. It wasn't just that she didn't like being alone. She could not stand being without Joe for even an hour or two without getting frightened and depressed. At first, an extra beer during the day helped. Then a can of beer was necessary every two or three hours. One day as she was buying food and diapers and the usual beer, her mind's eye remembered a nearby package store with Smirnoff vodka sale signs pasted in the window. She had Joe's fake I.D. cards they had both used for years. There was never a buying problem. And she had gotten really good at hiding bottles, the full vodka bottles at the back of drawers, on closet floors, and the empties in laundry baskets to be left eventually in supermarket recycling bins.

Now when Joe came home, the house spilled over with unwashed laundry and dirty dishes. The baby cried in her crib, wanting to be held, only Lara was too drunk to pay attention. His pretty wife, unkempt, was more and more often passed out on the couch, or if she was awake, stumbled uncertainly about the house. She didn't speak much. When she did, her speech was slurred, and she seemed to giggle a lot.

Joe poured himself a drink, even thought about going out to get some decent weed. If Lara could have a good time, so could he. They were still in their teens. Why shouldn't they have a good time? Sure they were married and had a baby. But they were still kids like all their friends, and for once, Joe wanted to forget about work and responsibility and party, too. The two of them had a really good time that night. They laughed together. They made love for the first time in a long time.

The next day, Joe went back to work.

Lara went back to drinking. She was soon unable to squeeze enough from the housekeeping money to pay for enough liquor to keep her from getting the shakes, from getting depressed. She had asked friends and family too many times for extra cash, so she couldn't go back to them anymore without having to answer too many questions.

Lara thought about her two friends from high school whose way of earning extra money had once horrified her, but now held the promise of not only more drinking but fun. It would mean company for her, what with Joe being gone twelve, often more, hours each day. And Joe didn't have to know, did he, how she spent her days.

Lara's friends helped her to buy the kind of make-up and clothes she would never before have dreamed of wearing. The friend who had her own child shared her sitter with Lara to mind Lara's baby along with her own.

Within a year, it was Lara who was earning the living— she told Joe she had found jobs cleaning houses for other women—while Joe stayed home with the crying baby. His once steady ways, his job, had all been lost when he had begun late-night partying with Lara.

What he didn't know was that Lara had entered hell.

Joe was too drunk to care.

Chapter Three
ADDICTION TO BEHAVIORS

What Is Addictive Behavior?

An addictive behavior is something you feel compelled to do over and over again. An addictive behavior is an action based on an emotional need, a mental obsession, and a physical compulsion to perform that behavior. And not just once, but again and again. You can tell you are addicted to something when you can't let go of the idea of it. We've already discussed alcoholism and drug addiction, the addictions that include the use of external substances to alter inner chemistry.

Addictive behaviors also involve the alteration of a person's inner brain and glandular chemistry, but by constant repetition of behaviors rather than drugs. People can over-stimulate their own brain chemistry through pleasure-producing repetitive actions like gambling, sex/romance, shopping, binge eating, too many hours watching television, playing TV games, surfing the Internet. These activities release the brain's endorphins too often, and can too often over-stimulate the pleasure circuits, so that the brain craves more and more of the activity just in order not to feel depressed.

An addictive behavior—like gambling, for instance—might begin as something to do for fun, or out of boredom, loneliness, frustration, or just a need to belong by behaving like a particular group at school or around the neighborhood.

But there are a couple of unforeseeable traps:

1. The adolescent brain has yet to finish maturing in the judgment areas of the frontal lobes, the brain's 'stop' or 'look before you leap' system. These frontal lobes will not finish maturing until the mid-twenties. The limbic system, on the other hand, the parts of the brain that promise rewards, is fully active. This means the temptation toward the immediate gratification, excitement, danger, general mayhem and risk-taking, from drugs to hang-gliding to unprotected sex is far more fascinating than worrying about long-term consequences.

2. The other traps, as we have already discussed, are genes and environment. The consequences of these are dangerous because they are so unpredictable. These two traps can be an easy out, however, as they need you and your behavior to activate them.

An addictive behavior might begin as just a momentary experiment among friends—everybody is out skateboarding for an hour and you do it for six hours. It might begin as part of a family activity like watching television too much, or eating too much fast food together. But what might begin as an ordinary pleasure or an experiment can turn into a compulsion so irresistible it wrecks a life.

An addictive behavior might also start, not from a pleasure, but from anxiety, from nervousness. Obsessive habits grow out of ordinary activities. Checking a couple of times that your spelling is correct, that everything is in its right place in your room, that your hands are clean and your hair exactly where it's supposed to be is normal. Checking over and over and over again can come from anxiety over having to do things and to have things just right. There can be a completion compulsion over chores, or homework, any kind of task. It's called perfectionism, but it is really conformity to what you've been told, so you don't stand out from the crowd, or get punished for anything undone or done wrong. The relief factor, the "everything's done and done right" moment can be addictive, too. Life may be in the details, but attention to the details of life does not mean getting stuck in them, or becoming obsessive over them.

- -

Observe Your Own Compulsions

1.   Do you check and recheck yourself in the mirror to see if your face, hair, body, clothes look all right?

2.   Do you double and triple check your list of friends to make sure you have enough?

3.   Do you have rituals that make you feel unsafe or uncomfortable if you break the pattern? The way you go to bed, the way your possessions occupy your room, the way you go to school, eat your food?

4.   Do you double and triple check your 'to-do' list because you are addicted to getting things done so you can feel safe and breathe free?

- -

Addictive Behavior Is Always Destructive

A behavior addict cannot do the thing she or he does only once. The behavior must be repeated over and over again. So an addictive behavior takes over the time needed to do other things, activities that are healthy, necessary for the totality of life lived with purpose and variety.

Also, because addictive, repetitive behaviors change the brain chemistry of the addict, once is never enough. For an addict, a single mall or Internet shopping spree, a single go at the quarter machine or Internet card game, a single candy bar or junk food binge, a single porn site visit or sex party, is never enough to satisfy the craving.

For a behavior addict, the destructiveness lies in the compulsive need to repeat and repeat the behavior. The trouble is, you never know whether you will get hooked the first time or the tenth, after one day or one year or five.

If the behavior is illegal, of course, it is even more destructive, such as underage drinking or drunk driving, underage gambling or Internet porn.

Recovery

The bad news: Addictive behaviors can cause life-changing disasters. They can lead to the onset of mental illness, like depression and anxiety disorders. Addictive behaviors can lead to health problems. Too much sitting around time watching television, playing video games, on the computer can lead to obesity or lack of necessary muscular development. Addictive behaviors can lead to dropping out of school or running away, whole ranges of crime and convictions—all to provide time and money to indulge the addictive behavior.

*THE GOOD NEWS...*We, alone among the species, can rise above our genes, our environments, our backgrounds, cultures, and conditioned responses.

We alone among species (that we know of) can be conscious of our behaviors through self-awareness, through self-observation, through talking with each other, teaching one another new ways of thinking and behaving. And through changing behavior, we change the neural pathways of the brain and create new pathways and new lives for ourselves.

As soon as you see yourself in the grip of any addictive behavior, first watch it for a while and learn its ways. Don't go into a state

We can rise above our genes, our environments, our backgrounds, cultures, and conditioned responses.

of denial or just accept that it's the way you are, or the way you have to stay. Admit it. Share the problem with someone you trust, a friend, a teacher, your parents if you can talk to them, school psychologists if not. But get help.

People can learn to identify and to reprogram their behaviors. Many treatment centers, support groups, programs are available to teach addicted people to recognize and overcome the powerful chemical signals that prompt them to use a substance or act on a behavior. You probably won't say to yourself, "Ah, there's the dopamine and serotonin and adrenalin rush." But when your heart pounds, your head feels light, your blood races, you feel heat in your middle, your eyes sharpen, your body trembles—you can bet you are in the grip of your very own high, produced by your very own chemicals—all of them prompting you to take the action that will up the rush, prolong the high, by the behavior that does this for you.

Support groups made up of other recovering addicts, who have been through everything you have, will teach you through sharing their own experiences, about the addictive disease you have, and the path of recovery. They have been through so much themselves, they'll see through your defenses or subterfuges, twistings of the truth and dodgings of the consequences—they have done it all. And because they have been there and back, they can help you and themselves spot the craving signals and stay clean and clear of not only addictive substances, but the behaviors that start you off on a destructive cycle.

Recovery is hard. But is there anything
harder than the life of an addict?

Watch Yourself for Two or Three Days

Pay attention to what things, people, activities you feel are so important, so necessary to you and your sense of happiness, pleasure, feeling good, that you believe you can't do without them.

We're not, of course, talking about the ordinary, intelligent activities of life, like brushing your teeth or doing homework or chores. These things, well done or even done at all, can give you a sense of order, safety from anxiety, or at least keep other people off your back.

We're talking about chosen pleasures, escapes, distractions, releases from stress. These could be anything from video games to being with a particular group of friends, a particular boyfriend/girlfriend, to eating a certain kind of food, watching familiar shows on television, hanging out in a particular place.

The repetition over and over again of all of these really favorite activities will change the nerve pathways of your brain and therefore your brain chemistry, the chemicals released into your brain and carried through the rest of your body. During favorite activities, you'll feel anything from a warm, familiar release of tension, to a real glow, to a rush from chemicals released not only in your brain but from the adrenal glands that sit on top of your liver. The adrenal glands store, synthesize, and release feel-good chemicals—dopamine, norepinephrine, and epinephrine. These send that feeling of happy excitement through your brain and body that counteracts whatever tension, anxiety, depression, boredom you might be feeling. You can understand from a biochemical explanation how repetitive behaviors change your brain/body chemistry.

After a period of time, days to weeks to months, you'll discover your brain/body has adjusted to the amount of pleasure you are giving it, and you need to spend more and more hours on these activities to maintain or increase the release of the pleasure chemicals. This is called progression. We develop a tolerance for the chemicals, either the outer chemicals taken into the body by substance addiction, or to our own internal chemicals to which we have become addicted that are released by the repetitive behaviors.

So just as alcoholic/addicts need more and more of what they use to maintain or increase their high, behavior addicts need to spend more and more hours on whatever behaviors they need to release their inner chemicals.

EXPERIMENT:
Are You a Behavior Addict?

If you want to test whether you are really addicted to a certain activity, person, place, thing, don't let yourself do it for a day or two. You'll feel anxious, incomplete, even depressed. Obviously, we have basic needs for food, supportive family and friends, air to breathe, in order to live healthy lives. But if you find you are desperate for something not actually necessary for mental and physical survival—to eat a Snickers bar or play a video game or shop, or be constantly with a particular boy or girlfriend—question the obsession to eat, to do, to possess, to stimulate your own chemistry by being with a particular person.

You don't have to do anything about these findings. Just observe what happens to you during these experiments in self-understanding to learn what you actually need, and what you only think you need to feel all right.

Sex and Romance Addiction

Along with alcohol and drugs, sex addiction and romance addiction (these can be two separate addictions) can get out of hand.

This is partly because humans keep their young infantilized (treat teens like babies) much longer than all other species so they can't marry when they mature sexually. Increasingly, as humans learn more, we need more years to pass on the knowledge necessary to function in our society. Bodies mature sexually in the teen years, but the brain's knowledge and judgment centers of the frontal cortex do not.

The physical capacity for the joy of sex is the greatest pleasure young humans know, with its rush of dopamine, serotonin, adrenaline, the highest of inner drugs. But sex gives us more. Sex is a total escape from ourselves, our loneliness and fear and other bad feelings. Sex gives us a momentary sense of power over another person, of someone's total attention, the satisfaction of the need to be loved and wanted, admired, in control of someone else, even if only for a moment. The need for one's emptiness to be filled, the need to be rescued—all are fulfilled for a little while. But it is one's own fantasy that's the turn-on, remember, not the other person. Just as it is one's own chemistry that is the turn-on, not the other person. A shock to learn this, but true anyway.

The Danger of Addiction Is Universal

If even ordinary comforts and pleasures like food and shopping, television and romance are addictive, you can imagine in yourself or observe in others, what an addiction to drugs, alcohol, or dangerous addictive behaviors can lead to.

Do You Have Any Addictions?

Other words for addictions that are often used by psychologists are dependencies when referring to drugs or alcohol, attachments when referring to people or particular places, obsessions and compulsions or compulsive behaviors when referring to activities.

The word used does not matter. Almost everybody but the most supremely well-adjusted among us has addictions, attachments, dependencies, compulsions of some kind—the feeling of being safe only when certain things and people and behaviors are clung to like life rafts. It is only when these interfere with or destroy people and their families, or create psychological or legal problems, that something has to be done about the destructive repeated behaviors. There is a big difference between taking one drink and getting drunk too often, just as there is a difference between being in love and stalking your lover everywhere and anywhere. What is always the most important thing is to pay attention to your own thoughts, feelings, and above all, behaviors, so that you do no harm—to yourself or anyone else.

- -

Can You List Your Addictions or Dependencies, Attachments, Obsessions in reference to:

People? _____

Activities? _____

Substances? _____

Places? _____

Things? _____

- -

STORY Romance Addict

Marlee and Sam were the most perfect couple in high school. Everybody said so.

Marlee was a junior, Sam a senior. Marlee had spent almost her entire junior year following Sam around. She went to every rehearsal of every play he was in, became a cheerleader for all his games, hung around the places in town where Sam was bound to turn up with his friends.

One day when everybody they knew was hanging out, crowded outside their favorite Starbucks, Marlee managed to snuggle up against him and look right up into his eyes.

"I think she's finally got you cornered," someone said, laughing.

Marlee chasing Sam had not gone unnoticed. But how would Sam react? Would he pull away, get angry at the teasing? Was this too public a moment for him?

But Sam had taken the moment—and Marlee—in his stride. He had laughed, put his arm around her, and simply swept Marlee along with him wherever their friends went. They were a couple at beach picnics, at backyard bonfires, at local fairs, at any party or game or dance that was happening. Of course, that included Sam's senior prom.

It was the most glorious night of Marlee's life. The lights, the music, the feel, the smell, the breath of Sam's body close to her, his eyes on her, his hands—Marlee needed no drink, no party drugs—her whole being was high, drunk, on fire from just being near Sam. She never wanted the ecstasy of this night to end.

There was only one thing wrong, missing, one small but entirely important omission on Sam's part that threatened Marlee's total happiness, her feeling that she would never be lonely again.

In all these months, and now, on this most important night of all, Sam had never said those magic words, "I love you, Marlee, and I want you to be my girlfriend from now on."

Nor did Sam call the next day, or the next, nor all the rest of the week. There were makeup exams, end of the year craziness—Marlee knew how to invent excuses for him. She had become an expert in inventing excuses for Sam's evasiveness in the face of verbal commitment for months. His calls were always less frequent after her particularly emotionally intense evenings like the night of Sam's senior prom. She was never sure that he felt as intense as she did, but she knew he felt her intensity and needed time, some space, to recover from intimate moments.

The scenes began the first time Sam picked her up to join everyone at the coffee shop.

"Sam, tell me you love me," Marlee burst out before she could stop herself the minute they were alone in Sam's car.

"Hey, sweetie, you know I don't say things like that." Sam kept his tone light, but his mouth tightened. Marlee knew it was a warning sign to drop the intensity.

"Then just tell me you feel about me the way I feel about you." She couldn't help it. She had to go on. She could hear the begging tone in her voice. She couldn't help that, either. All the months of being a pretty, happy, willing companion seemed suddenly to melt away in a needy, grasping desperation to belong to Sam, to have Sam belong exclusively to her. Her passionate desperation frightened her. No wonder it scared Sam.

"I'm not sure I do feel the same way," said Sam. His voice was careful, a bit hardened. "I like you a lot, Marlee. You're a great girl, you know that. We have fun together."

Sam had been seeing her exclusively for almost a year. He took her to his senior prom. And this is all he can say to her?

"Fun! Is that all I mean to you? Fun?"

"Honey, I'm no good at being intense, you know that. We've had a great time together. We can go on having a great time together. Now, can we drop this and go for coffee with the others?"

Marlee's heart stopped. Her blood refused to circulate. Her whole body went cold.

"There's someone else," she said, and she could hear her own voice, cold, hard, tight. "You've got another girl-friend."

"You're being nuts," said Sam.

Marlee flung herself out of the car and walked home.

For the next three weeks, Marlee called, texted, wrote letters. Sam returned none of her frantic messages of apology. Questioning his friends, she discovered he was off rock-climbing, but not with whom.

She sought him out all summer in their old familiar places along the beach, at the movies, in coffeehouses, at the mall, all to no avail.

But it wasn't until the night she found herself going through his family's trash at two o'clock in the morning searching for any clue, any sign of another girl—makeup, tights, hair clips—his mother wore none of these things—that Marlee realized in horror what she had become.

Chapter Four

ADDICTION
TO OURSELVES

Mostly We Are Addicted to Ourselves

Above all, we are addicted to ourselves.

We are addicted to our own self-importance, and this may be the most dangerous addiction of all if it is not understood properly. Self-importance physically is based on the oldest of evolution's laws: survive, don't die, STAY ALIVE!

The dangerous part of self-importance is not the physical, but the psychological addiction to ourselves. Addiction is the needing more and more of something to feel all right, to feel safe, to make fear, depression, and anxiety go away. It may begin with the evolutionary imperative LIFE MUST LIVE—but then it translates itself into I MUST LIVE AND TO LIVE I MUST HAVE IMPORTANCE SO THE GROUP WILL PROTECT ME.

So we grow more and more addicted to our own self-importance. By the time we grow into adults of our species, we are all puffed out with ourselves. We have become addicted to our own colors and nationalities, our own opinions, to other people's opinions of us and our popularity, our images of ourselves, our own personal security, to what belongs to us, to our own ideas of how the world and people should be. We are addicted to our own need for security, acceptance, addicted to our own people, family, cultures, homes, to our own possessions.

We think we need to defend all this to stay alive. It's what we've been taught at home, at school, by our leaders. Killer competition may have been necessary 40,000 years ago in the Stone Age when food was scarce, the getting of it dangerous, and the only place to live was a dark and freezing cave. The trouble is, we are still functioning with that Stone Age brain, when a lot of us now have supermarkets and central heating, and if we could learn to share instead of grab and defend, there would be plenty to go around on this Earth. Sadly, we haven't considered this yet, so the fear of losing what we have, of not getting enough, turns us into greedy addicts.

The problem of addiction is: How much is enough? It's when we want more than enough that addiction sets in.

Fear is the beginning of addiction. Once an evolutionary genetic survival tool among many others, fear rather than intelligence can take over the brain and dictate our thoughts and behavior.

Interesting Questions

How many habits, daily rituals, how much stuff, how many friends, possessions could you let go of and still feel safe?

Which views of the world, your family, culture, religion, other people and their colors, countries, religions, money, class, ethnic backgrounds could you change and still feel secure?

- -

The problem of addiction is: How much is enough? It's when we want more than enough that addiction sets in.

- -

Addiction Is Dependency

It's the fear in dependency that breeds pain, the fear of the loss of what we depend on, whether that's a drug or a boyfriend or an achievement. This fear of loss, of not getting enough, then breeds anger. We get angry at who or what we depend on—the threat of loss can create great rage.

We confuse love and dependency. Love is a state of being, a state of having and being enough inside yourself so that you have plenty of energy and affection to give out to the world. Dependency is the need to take in. When dependency on people, with its needs and demands, its fears and its anger, comes in one window, love, that state of generous affection and goodwill, flies out the other. We are not each other's to suck the blood from, like vampires. We are not meant to cling obsessively to any relationship with family, country, lovers, or friends, in an effort to save ourselves from fear or loneliness. Clutch too tightly—everyone chokes.

Addiction is an imperative need: a chemical, psychological, emotional, mental, and physical need. Addiction is dependency, fear, and anger. Dependency on something outside us to soothe us, to save us from pain and loneliness, to reassure us that we are alive, that we belong to the pack (evolutionarily humans are a pack animal, not loners), especially that we matter, is an evolutionary trait inherited from our animal past. Physical dependencies exist. Psychological dependencies are not necessary.

Mental Pre-dispositions to Self-Addiction

GENETIC EVOLUTION

Once the evolutionary problems of fright and dependency are looked at as the genetic basis for addiction, there are also the further complex problems of mental illnesses now so evident among teenagers.

The process of evolution, according to the great modern evolutionary scientists like Richard Dawkins (*The Selfish Gene*) and Stephen Jay Gould (*Full House*), suggests that the best adapted of the species (the smart ones that handled their environment best) mated with each other and passed on their genes. Smart survival often depended back in the Stone Age on being so neurotic you jumped at every noise, grabbed every opportunity to con, steal, or beat your neighbor out of his goods. You had to be obsessive about staying alive to stay alive.

So, evolutionary genetic chemistry can also account for obsessive ideas and compulsive behaviors. Our overeating, shopping, gambling, risk-taking, sex-addicted teens are simply behaving like our caveman/woman ancestors—even when the need to behave

that way is no longer necessary. In point of fact, there is plenty of food and clothing to serve the whole world, if we could only learn to share instead of grab, rape, and kill. To wake up to these facts is humanity's most important task.

Note: if we change our behavior, it changes the neural pathways of our brains. Just as certain drugs like heroin permanently alter our brains, repeated behavior and ideas can permanently change our brains—for better or worse.

CULTURE

Culture, by which we mean what everybody around us is doing and thinking and talking about, also conditions us. Think of human beings, for a moment, as rats in a cage.

Teens have grown up seeing their parents live in unconscious dependence. They depend on their money, their sense of their own importance, their success or lack of it, for their sense of security. They may depend on drugs or alcohol. They depend on their images of themselves in the community, their power in their families. Too many adults depend on their children's accomplishments for their happiness instead of on themselves and their own lives. These teens will have learned to depend as well. Too often, all teens do is rebel, basing their lives, if not on their parents' lives, on a negative blueprint of those lives. This is not the same as understanding the human brain's search for security and getting over the idea that there is any such thing as security, or that the brutality of dependency can work in any way.

The results of living dependently (the need for approval, for power) are grinding us down—peer pressure, poverty and homelessness, drug addiction, behavioral addiction, incarceration, mental

We must be psychologically free to be happy and not suffer the pangs of psychological dependency.

and physical illness, war and murder—everywhere there are examples of getting through life by depending on external factors for security. We have evolved physically as group mammals—we depend on the Web for information, or the mall to shop, we need each other for body warmth. But we must stand alone psychologically. We must be psychologically free to be happy and not suffer the pangs of psychological dependency.

Note: As we have discovered, since there is no security, the only way to live securely is to learn to live well and happily without it.

THE HUMAN BRAIN

We're also frightened psychologically because the human brain, among all the species, has not only a consciousness, but a self-consciousness. No animal but human beings projects its own future, and the terror of that future makes us want to escape into anything from drugs to movies to mayhem, from politics to money, from sports to living through other human beings. Then we become dependent on those escapes and grow even more afraid of their loss.

Brain scientists like Steven Pinker and Daniel Dennett, philosophers like J. Krishnamurti and David Hume, reveal the brain's best-kept secret. There is no part of the brain that is the self. No MRI can find a self. Many places in the brain, especially those that create and retain memories, all contribute to and create continuity, the 'story of me', to give us a sense of security. Look down your shirt. Is anyone really home? We all feel as if there were an emptiness, a hole in us, something not solid—you're not alone in this. Another instance of how connected, how much the same all human beings are. But it's scary to understand this, to know that our selves are just made of our own recorded memories, and there's no real 'I'.

It will also save you—this understanding. After all, it's only into an empty glass that anything can be poured: Love, God, the Intelligence of the Universe. We are so afraid of the death of the 'me'—this mythical beast that doesn't even exist—we spend our lives trying to protect it, make it bigger, defend it from attack by ideas different from our own.

If you let it, not your body but your 'me', die now, and again whenever it arises, you won't suffer from hurt feelings, psychological fear, and the painful results of all those escape addictions and dependencies. *After all, since it's only the 'me' that's hurt, and there really is no 'me'—what can hurt you?*

Questions:

What views, opinions, ideas about life, people, work, the world, money, religion, God, love, good and evil, do you think define you? List some of these as an exercise in understanding yourself and the thought patterns in your brain, your belief systems.

What people define you?
Who is important in your life and why?

_____

_____

_____

_____

_____

_____

_____

_____

_____

_____

All these things can become dependencies.
And dependencies are prisons.

Reminders

1. "An addict is any person who has become physically or emotionally chemically dependent," say Bettie and Jennifer Youngs, authors of *A Teen's Guide to Living Drug-Free.*

This is true whether the dependency is on a substance or a behavior or another person. Withdrawal, being deprived of the needed substance or behavior or person, causes physical and mental suffering.

2. The American Medical Association in 1956 first defined addiction as a disease, not a lack of will power.

3. In their book *Addiction*, Hoffman and Froemke state "any so-called lack of will-power in an addict has been caused by changes in the brain. Dependence on drugs or alcohol caused these very changes." Addiction is "a chronic, relapsing brain disease," they add.

Treatment consists of therapy, sometimes medication to restore the brain's normal functions, and always ongoing support groups for human community, affection, role-modeling, and above all the dialogue of self-investigating and self-understanding.

Understanding How to Live

"Understanding how to live is the purpose of life, to free the mind from pain, dependency, illness, its own conditioned habits, so that the joy of connection to one another and the universe is possible... Psychological suffering is self-absorbing; love can only happen in the absence of self. It is insight into one's self and its ways that ends suffering," says Hannah Carlson, M.Ed., LPC in her book *The Courage to Lead: Start your Own Support Group, Mental Illnesses and Addiction.*

Recovery is to look at the ways of your self and to stop doing whatever hurts you or anyone else.

THE TEEN BRAIN

In *The Teen Brain Book* by Dale Carlson, there is this section on teen survival.

Surviving Adolescence Well

We all get older if we don't get dead. We survive the teenage years sooner or later and find ourselves by twenty or twenty-one launched into the world of college, professions, marriage, jobs, careers, all that. Whether we actually mature enough to handle all this properly or not is based on two basic conditions.

1. Proper biophysical development of body and especially the prefrontal cortex, the CEO of our judgment, plans, behaviors, decisions, moral and ethical positions that allow us to control impulses, measure consequences, and live to good purpose.

2. Paying close attention to the conditioned, knee-jerk reactions of thought and feeling and behavior and learning to stop at the source whatever will hurt ourselves or others. The conditioned thoughts and feelings may not go away, but maturity is based on not acting them out, and on behavior that is good for all, not just for the self.

You can decide whether to become one of those tragic infantile adults who blame and whine, abuse sex or drugs or children, yell, hurt other people whenever they get frightened or upset; or to be happy. It's freeing to know it isn't what cards you're dealt that decides your life, it's what you understand about the game and how you play it.

Because most people are never taught how the human brain works, our brains scare us. We never learn that:

1. While thought chatters, the background condition of the mind is to be empty. We get so frightened at the emptiness we fill it with all kinds of destructive escapes.

2. We invent a self, like a package with all its contents, to fill up the emptiness and then believe in it and get upset when every few seconds the normal emptiness comes back.

In short, we frighten ourselves due to the fear and simple empty moments that are part of just having a human brain.

Mental Health

The most basic definition of a mentally healthy person is one whose psyche can cope with internal and external reality well enough to get through life without harming itself or anyone else, or suffering so much that ordinary functioning in relationship to yourself, other people, and your work is disrupted. The ability to handle nondestructively whatever stress life hands you is the mark of a mentally healthy person.

Addiction to Yourself

Addicts, and in many ways all of us, are addicted to their own chemistry. We are convinced we love our lovers, friends, activities, but just as with alcohol and drugs, what we love is how all these things and people make us feel and what they do to our chemistry.

The only

way to feel

secure is to

learn to live

insecurely.

Pay attention to your own body, the way your chemistry makes you feel, the high you get when your boyfriend or girlfriend looks at you a certain way or the low when they aren't there at all. Pay attention to when you are deprived of a video game or a party because of homework or punishment. Pay attention to your chemistry and how you feel when there are any changes in your life, even small ones. Feel a chemistry change when you have to get out of bed, leave a room, can't go out with a friend. Butterflies, a pain in the chest, holding the breath, agitation, all these are chemical changes. Watch your own mood/chemical reactions for two or three days and see what you find out about your own personal chemistry.

Another source of chemical highs and lows to attend to are personal accomplishments, money or empty pockets, new possessions, or wanting something. All this hanging on to things, groups, ideas, people, behaviors, are addictions to your own chemical reactions to them.

NOTE: There is no such thing as security, no matter what most people seem to hope for: everything comes and goes, life flows with good and bad events. So the only way to feel secure is to learn to live insecurely, with no dependencies, no addictions, no habits of thought, feeling, behaviors, no dependency on people, places, things, substances, holding everything that comes to you with open hands.

Talk to Each Other

It isn't just you. Most of us don't know how to be in this world, how to behave. So our eyes just stare out suspiciously in the dark, like animals on night roads, and all we see is other eyes staring back.

Who likes us? Who is on our side? Who'll speak to us? Who won't?

Anything that takes the edge off this haunting terror, the evolutionary terror of being all alone out there—in school, on the streets, even in the family and among friends—is welcome. Addictions and dependencies turn out not to work. What does work is talking to each other and finding out we're all in the same boat.

Actually, each of us is alone in our own skins. No point in fighting it, hiding from it, escaping it. We each have to live out our own lives. But because we are all in the same boat, we can hold hands, talk to each other about the best ways of handling life when it comes at you, and keep each other company. As we've said, all human brains are pretty much alike.

> *We're all scared we won't be accepted.*
> *We all beat on ourselves for not measuring up.*
> *Or gossip, beating up on others.*
> *Or step on each other and call this competition.*

Then, exhausted because nothing has changed, we try to escape in all the ways we've been discussing.

You start talking about all this, and what you'll see is other heads nodding at you, knowing just exactly what you're talking about. It's the best cure for feeling all alone out there human beings have invented yet.

Again, Why Bother?

It's not a question of just being a good girl or a good boy that you learn to live without addiction to substances, behaviors, to your self. If you aren't going to kill yourself today, you might as well live wisely—which is, with the least amount of pain and the most joy.

The deal is, to be alive is to be uncomfortable! Joy happens, but not predictably, and it's based on decent, intelligent behavior. It is not based on what you think. Our minds are like monkeys always jumping around a cage, from one thought to another, full of all the voices of everybody you ever knew, and all the things that have happened to you, and all the things you just think have happened to you. Brain scientists have begun to understand we edit and reconstruct our memories. So thought, while it can be reliable technologically, is never reliable psychologically.

It comes back to the fact that it's how you behave that matters. And while some behaviors may bring instant relief or escape from pain, the addictive behaviors always have horrid consequences, and there is, as we have said before, a terrible price for selling yourself out. Not just jail, insanity, or death in the case of drugs. Not just mental and psychological oblivion in the case of addictive thought and behavior. The price you pay is your life.

Addictive behaviors always have horrid consequences, and there is a terrible price for selling yourself out.

And the System Will Kill You if You Don't Kill Yourself

People are afraid of alcoholics and addicts and those with mental illness. Society has a tendency to judge them undesirable, overmedicate them into zombies, and lock them up, as if the punishment of prison, locked wards, and psychiatric medications will change what is happening to teenagers. In many cases, cognitive/behavioral therapy is offered, but basically teenagers are told to shape up or else.

Social psychologist James Rapuano works in the field of correctional counseling in the criminal justice system. In an astute report, he writes:

"The current trend in the field of correctional counseling has refocused its objectives from punitive to therapeutic. The 'nothing works, why bother' attitude, and the 1980's punitive sanctions of 'tail them, nail them, jail them' to protect the community and public safety, has faded in favor of the 1960's'approach when the youth culture openly rebelled against traditional social values. The therapeutic approach plus psychotropic medications to adjust brain chemistry is the current trend."

The difficulty, says Rapuano, is that when released, the teen patient/client will return to his former neighborhood and friends, and again engage in illegal activities and again be returned to the criminal justice system.

The further difficulty is that eventually, of course, the teenager will not 'age-out' of criminal activity after the teen years. For males this criminal behavior is usually centered on property crimes and theft. In females, sexual promiscuity, and in later years, 'borderline personality'.

Clearly, neither incarceration nor the combination of psychiatric medication and present cognitive behavior communication between patient and clinician in the criminal justice system is working well for teenagers.

Something more is needed, says Rapuano. Perhaps an answer to their question: Why should they change? We want a conclusion to their problems so they no longer infect the community. But we don't tell them why, or what's in it for them.

Can We Evolve from Human to Humane?

Recovery, not just from addictions but all kinds of nasty ancestral inherited behaviors, is necessary if the human race is going to survive, since everything in the universe, and everyone, according to the laws of physics, affects everything and everyone else.

Our animal inheritance of self-centered self-preservation doesn't have to be our destiny. The human brain is plastic; it can change. We can observe what we're doing and stop it. We can create our own joy by letting the brain produce endorphins, its own opiate-like chemicals. We can learn to cooperate, not compete. It begins with understanding ourselves, our heritage and culture and behavior, all our knee-jerk reactions and evolutionary habits—and stopping them.

Since humans did not create the universe and its contents, we may not ever be able to understand our place, or our part, in the whole.

What we can do is understand ourselves, our own nature, and our effect on ourselves and each other. Just this much, like everything else, will affect the entire universe.

STORY Two Addicts in Love

The night of the Homecoming Dance was also the night of the beginning of the end of Alex's life. He and his friends had brought their dates to a club only New York's richest kids could afford—on someone's father's credit card.

The music was loud, the dancing frenzied, and the lights spun drunkenly in the vast darkness.

And there she was, small, delicate, expensively dressed, standing slightly apart from the crowd she had come in with—a class younger than Alex's in the same exclusive prep school.

Alex's world stopped, his whole being riveted to this glorious girl. Even knowing she was beyond his grasp, forbidden to him by family wealth and social position, he moved through the club's mayhem until he was close enough to touch her.

Dana, already high on vodka and whatever else was going around among her friends at the club, succumbed to Alex's charm, his very evident attraction to her, and her boredom with her own set.

"They won't let me date you," Dana told Alex as they moved, body to body to the heat of the music and the night and each other.

"My parents won't like this either," Alex said. It wasn't easy for his parents to meet the expensive prep school tuition, and they hoped their son would use his schooling, not to waste time on a girl, but to find a place in the world better than their own.

They were crazy about each other, but it was clear Dana was inviting Alex into her world, not planning to enter his. And Alex moved up from beer and bowling on Saturday nights to the parties given by Dana and her set.

Dana and her set did not drink beer.

The supply of drugs was as endless, as varied as their dates, their evenings of lovemaking, the private parties in private clubs, aboard yachts, in luxurious East Side apartments. Dana's crowd had local dealers for their marijuana, cocaine, and heroin. They used Cyber-dealers for their Vicodin and oxycodone, Ecstasy, K. There were their parents' private stashes for whenever they ran out of anything.

Alex got high on drugs, higher on Dana, all through his senior year. He went crazy with jealousy when her parents insisted she attend coming-out balls, country club dances, formal family and social occasions to which she was not allowed to invite him. He went crazy when they took her off to Europe, on cruises, hoping she would pull herself together, forget Alex, and meet someone of her own social standing.

Often on weekends, she would escape a formal dance early, and meet Alex where he waited in his father's old car parked in the lamp-lit, New York street below.

By the end of Dana's junior year, Dana was no longer being taken on cruises. She was being sent to expensive rehabs. She had begun to use heroin more and more often, quicker, higher highs, she said. After a while she was using the needle, at first once, then twice a week, then more.

"What are you doing to yourself, to us?"

Alex held her thinner, trembling body close to him.

"I can't stop," Dana said. "It's not even the high any more. I get so sick when I'm not using. My bones hurt, my back, my insides shake. I'm too scared to stop now."

"If this is how you're going to go, I'm going with you," Alex whispered.

Dana went to more expensive rehabilitation hospitals.

But for Alex there were no rehabs, and there was no college after prep school. Without resources, Alex learned to survive and feed his heroin addiction any way he could. He dealt drugs in Needle Park, in the shadows of Manhattan's street corners, slept rough on the benches and in the wild undergrowth of Central Park, eating when he could swallow, from the trash containers in the Central Park Mall and near the children's playgrounds. He was too ashamed to go home, ask for help. He dreamed when he was drunk or high enough of kicking it, making good, claiming Dana once more as his own.

SECTION TWO
Self-Test Questions

OBSESSIVE-COMPULSIVE DISORDER

OCD Screening Checklist

Copyright, J. H. Greist, J. W. Jefferson, I. M. Marks.
American Psychiatric Press, 1986.

1. Do you have thoughts that bother you or make you anxious and that you can't get rid of regardless of how hard you try?

2. Do you have a tendency to keep things extremely clean or to wash your hands very frequently, more than other people you know?

3. Do you check things over and over to excess?

4. Do you have to straighten, order, or tidy things so much that it interferes with other things you want to do?

5. Do you worry excessively about acting or speaking more aggressively than you should?

6. Do you have great difficulty discarding things even when they have no practical value?

People with OCD usually have difficulty with some of the following activities. Answer each question by circling the appropriate number next to it.

0   *No problem with activity—takes me same time as average person. I do not need to repeat or avoid it.*

1   *Activity takes me twice as long as most people, or I have to repeat it twice, or I tend to avoid it.*

2   *Activity takes me three times as long as most people, or I have to repeat it three or more times ritually, or I usually avoid it.*

Score			Activity
0	1	2	Taking a bath/shower
0	1	2	Washing dishes
0	1	2	Turning lights and taps on or off
0	1	2	Mailing letters
0	1	2	Form filing
0	1	2	Washing hands/face
0	1	2	Handling/cooking food
0	1	2	Locking or closing doors or windows
0	1	2	Reading
0	1	2	Care of hair (washing, combing, brushing)
0	1	2	Cleaning house
0	1	2	Using electrical appliances, heaters
0	1	2	Writing
0	1	2	Brushing teeth
0	1	2	Keeping things tidy
0	1	2	Doing arithmetic or accounts
0	1	2	Getting to work
0	1	2	Dressing and undressing
0	1	2	Bed making, going to bed
0	1	2	Doing own work

0	1	2	Cleaning shoes
0	1	2	Touching door handles
0	1	2	Using toilet to urinate
0	1	2	Using toilet to defecate
0	1	2	Touching own genitals, petting, or sexual intercourse
0	1	2	Throwing things away
0	1	2	Visiting a hospital
0	1	2	Washing clothing
0	1	2	Handling waste or waste bins
0	1	2	Touching people or being touched

results

Total Scores: ■10 increase the possibility of obsessive-compulsive disorder (OCD), and further evaluation is recommended. Total scores ■20 are highly suggestive of OCD.

STORY Living In Terror

Since my earliest memory of being afraid, I can recall a ritual or "special" way of thinking or acting.

I think I may have been about five years old when my fears and then my rituals began. My family—my mother, father and older brother—had just moved to a new and much larger New York City apartment from our small, sunny apartment where I had shared a room with my brother. My new home was in a darker, older building, and I didn't like the way it smelled. I was assigned to my own room, to me a separate cell, for the first time. It did not face outward over the quiet, tree-lined street as the other bedrooms did, but looked out into shadows. Out of my window, I could see the courtyard, big enough to be inviting for a young child to play in, so small, however, that I could see across into neighbors' windows. Frightened, I understood that meant they could see into mine!

For me, special routines equal safety. I had my special way to enter the room. Dare not to touch the threshold with my foot! Step over and into the room, and on to the carpet. As I grew, my obsessional worries and fears fed off of my increasing knowledge and experience of my environment and the world at large. Among my fears was that an evil neighbor would extend a plank long enough to reach my window and use it to cross over the courtyard and invade my room at night. Although we lived on the third floor, and I never actually experienced anyone looking into my room, I lived in nightly fear of such an intrusion. I remember forcing my own compliance in the performance of different tasks in a specific sequence of steps. Whenever I missed a step or dropped what I was holding, I became so enraged that on occasion the only means of relief was to hit or scratch myself to release the fury and begin again. I waited to go to sleep until my digital clock read 11:11 p.m., in the hope of having less psychological torment the next day.

My obsessions served as my judge, jury, and prison guard. They determined my guilt and sentence for a crime I felt I must have committed without knowing when or what it was. As prison guard, my obsessions kept me so scared of being in or causing pain, that I stayed true to my compulsive rituals. I struggled to get through school. Anxiety is intensely distracting. Rather than being able to focus in class or on my homework, I worried constantly over what I myself or others meant when they spoke. I worried whether I, or someone else had been intentionally or unintentionally cruel. I agonized over not fitting in and not knowing how to be comfortable in my own skin, while I watched others make their transition through the normal adolescent crises of their teenage years with comparative ease.

I have few college memories. Those I do have are covered in a film of obsessive anxiety and isolation. I could just about sit through class before I was totally enveloped in panic and needed to retreat back to my dorm room. I developed an eating disorder to add to my psychological pain and anxiety. I binged and purged what I ate. I spent endless hours from early evening into the early morning examining my skin for defects. I tweezed, pulled, and picked at hair and bumps until my face was red and swollen. I self-medicated my tormenting loneliness and tried to relieve my frantic anxieties with drugs, alcohol, excessive spending, and lovers. The relief granted for short intervals would have been worth the price I had to pay for these indulgences, only I became addicted to what I thought of as vices. In an effort to control my obsessional worries and compulsions, my life had become completely unmanageable. I avoided people, places, and things that caused my anxiety or triggered my obsessions. I existed on the periphery of social and academic life, too afraid to be exposed to situations that might set off my panic, always wanting to have an easy exit to the sanctuary of my dorm room, the private life of my mind and rituals.

I managed nevertheless to earn graduate degrees and licensing in my field. There was now some degree of intervening respite from compulsive behavior and addiction.

My symptoms returned with a vengeance several months after the birth of my second child. I developed a new set of terrors. My fears of harming the children, or of others harming the children, was so intense that I would be awakened by the slightest sounds in a house I had lived in peacefully for five years. I was driven to check locks, oven knobs, windows, and the basement. I began to allow both of my children to sleep in my bed at night so that I could keep a vigilant watch over their rising and lowering chests.

So obsessively terrified was I that I might jerk the steering wheel off the road while driving them home one night, that I finally sought treatment at the Yale University Clinical Depression Study. I knew I was depressed. I had no idea until I was diagnosed, that I had OCD, obsessive-compulsive disorder.

While I was resistant to the use of antidepressant medication, I was willing to try anything that might help restore me to sanity. After several trials, we found a level of medication that relieved the grip of obsessional thinking and compulsive behavior on my life. I applied behavioral therapy techniques and a twelve-step program that provided me with the support, the psychological tools, and a new way of living—all necessary to keep me free from the shackles of my depression, anxiety, and OCD. As long as I follow the steps in the program and take my medication, I am granted a daily reprieve from my mental illness.

ALCOHOLISM

Screening for Problem Drinking

A.A. Grapevine, Inc. A.A. World Services, Inc. ©1973.

1. Have you ever decided to stop drinking
    for a week or so, but only lasted for a
    couple of days?   ❏ Yes   ❏ No

2. Do you wish people would mind their
    own business about your drinking—
    stop telling you what to do?   ❏ Yes   ❏ No

3. Have you ever switched from one
    kind of drink to another in the hope
    that this would keep you from
    getting drunk?   ❏ Yes   ❏ No

4. Have you had to have an
    eye-opener upon awakening
    during the past year?   ❏ Yes   ❏ No

5. Do you envy people who can drink
    without getting into trouble?   ❏ Yes   ❏ No

6. Have you had problems connected
    with drinking during the past year?   ❏ Yes   ❏ No

7.   Has your drinking caused trouble
      at home?   ❏ Yes   ❏ No

8.   Do you ever try to get "extra"
      drinks at a party because you
      do not get enough?   ❏ Yes   ❏ No

9.   Do you tell yourself you can stop
      drinking any time you want to, even
      though you keep getting drunk
      when you don't mean to?   ❏ Yes   ❏ No

10.   Have you missed days of work or
      school because of drinking?   ❏ Yes   ❏ No

11.   Do you have "blackouts"?   ❏ Yes   ❏ No
      (a "blackout" is when we have been drinking
      hours or days which we cannot remember.)

12.   Have you ever felt that your life would
      be better if you did not drink?   ❏ Yes   ❏ No

results

- -

If you answered **YES** to four or more questions, you are probably
in trouble with alcohol.

- -

A "blackout" is when we have been drinking hours or days which we cannot remember.

ANXIETY DISORDER

Anxiety Screening Test

Copyright, Benjamin J. Sadock. M.D. and Waguih William IsHak, M.D. New York University Department of Psychiatry, 1996.

Please answer Yes or No to the following questions:

1. Do you feel that you worry excessively about many things?   ❏ Yes   ❏ No

2. Do you experience sensations of shortness of breath, palpitations or shaking while at rest?   ❏ Yes   ❏ No

3. Do you have a fear of losing control of yourself or of "going crazy"?   ❏ Yes   ❏ No

4. Do you avoid social situations because of feelings of fear?   ❏ Yes   ❏ No

5. Do you have specific fears of certain objects, e.g., animals or knives?   ❏ Yes   ❏ No

6. Do you feel afraid that you will be in a place or a situation from which you feel that you will not be able to escape?   ❏ Yes   ❏ No

7.   Does the idea of leaving home
     frighten you?   ❑ Yes   ❑ No

8.   Do you have recurrent thoughts
     or images in your head that refuse
     to go away?   ❑ Yes   ❑ No

9.   Do you feel compelled to perform
     certain behaviors repeatedly e.g.,
     checking that you locked the doors
     or turned off the gas?   ❑ Yes   ❑ No

10. Do you persistently relive an
     upsetting event from the past?   ❑ Yes   ❑ No

results

The more you have answered **YES** to any of these questions, the more serious your problem may be. Please consult with a physician or licensed mental health professional experienced in diagnosing and treating anxiety.

DEPRESSION

The Hands Depression Screening Questionnaire

Copyright, President and Fellows of Harvard College and the National Mental Illness Screening Project, 1998

Fill in the response for each item based upon how you have been feeling for the past 2 weeks or longer. Scores do not confirm a diagnosis of depression. They do give an indication of what depression symptoms are like. It is recommended that you be evaluated by a licensed mental health professional for a more thorough and accurate assessment for a diagnosis.

**Over the past two weeks,
how often have you:**

	NONE	SOME	MOST	ALL
1. been feeling low in energy, slowed down?	❏	❏	❏	❏
2. been blaming yourself for things?	❏	❏	❏	❏
3. had poor appetite? or binges?	❏	❏	❏	❏
4. had difficulty falling asleep, staying asleep?	❏	❏	❏	❏

	NONE	SOME	MOST	ALL
5. been feeling hopeless about the future?	❏	❏	❏	❏
6. been feeling sick?	❏	❏	❏	❏
7. been feeling no interest in things?	❏	❏	❏	❏
8. had feelings of worthlessness?	❏	❏	❏	❏
9. thought about or wanted to commit suicide?	❏	❏	❏	❏
10. had difficulty concentrating or making decisions?	❏	❏	❏	❏

results

Score horizontally each question by determining the numerical value for each answer given using the following values:

NONE or little of the time = 0
SOME of the time = 1
MOST of the time = 2
ALL of the time = 3

Score vertically all of the total values to obtain your total score.

Score 0-8: Symptoms are not consistent with a major depressive episode. Presence of a major depressive episode is unlikely. A complete evaluation is not recommended except in the case of a positive response to the suicide question (item 9).

Score 9-16: Symptoms are consistent with a major depressive episode. Presence of a major depressive episode is likely. A complete evaluation is recommended. Severity level is typically mild or moderate, depending upon the degree of impairment.

Score 17-20: Symptoms are strongly consistent with criteria for a major depressive episode. Presence of major depressive episode is very likely. A complete evaluation is strongly recommended. In this higher range, the severity level may be more severe and require immediate attention.

EATING DISORDERS

The Eating Disorders Self Tests
Copyright © 1996, Mass Market Paperback. The Thin Disguise.
Pam Vredevelt, Dr. Deborah Newman, Dr. Harry Beverly, Dr. Frank Minirth

Place a check next to each statement that is true for you.

❏   I have fasted to lose weight.

❏   I feel guilty when I eat.

❏   To control my weight, I purge and/or take laxatives/diuretics.

❏   I am never satisfied with myself.

❏   The number on the scales determines whether a day will be good or bad.

❏   I feel fat even though people say I'm thin.

❏   I have stolen food, diet pills, or laxatives.

❏   I am obsessive about food, i.e.; recipes, cookbooks, calories, etc.

❏   I binge on a regular basis.

❏   I'm afraid of losing control when I eat.

❏   I have the "all or nothing" feeling.

❑   I have rituals when I eat.

❑   I feel guilty and fear gaining weight if I miss exercising
     or eat as much as one bite more than I planned.

❑   I lie about what I eat.

❑   I hide my food.

❑   My menstrual periods have ceased or are irregular.

results

A **YES** to any of the questions may indicate the start of a problem. The more you have yes answers to, the more serious your
problem may be. Please consult with a physician or mental health
counselor familiar with Eating Disorders. Continue with the *Perfectionism Scale*.

Perfectionism Scale

Fill in the blank with the number that best describes how you think most of the time.

1 = Never 2 = Rarely 3 = Sometimes 4 = Often

1. If I don't set the highest standards for myself, I am likely to end up a second-rate person. _____

2. People will probably think less of me if I make a mistake. _____

3. If I cannot do something really well, there is little point in doing it at all. _____

4. I should be upset if I make a mistake. _____

5. If I try hard enough, I should be able to excel at anything I attempt. _____

6. It is shameful for me to display weaknesses or foolish behavior. _____

7. I shouldn't have to repeat the same mistakes many times. _____

8. An average performance is bound to be unsatisfying to me. _____

9.   Failing at something important means
      I'm less of a person.   _____

10.   If I scold myself for failing to live up to
      expectations, it will help me to do better
      in the future.   _____

results

Add up the scores. The total may generally be interpreted as follows:

10-20   Non-perfectionistic
21-30   Average tendencies toward perfectionism
31-40   Very perfectionistic

If you scored in the high range, you may wish to consult with a licensed mental health professional for further evaluation.

STORY I'll Never Be Fat Again

My first thought, when I got to college, was not about the challenge of the classes ahead of me, the boys I would date, or the thrill of football weekends. It was, "I'll never be fat again."

I could control my eating now. I could count every calorie and, by the use of laxatives, I could rid my body of any excessive foods I may have consumed.

It was to be my revenge on my mother that I would never exceed a twenty-four inch waist, or a thirty-four inch hip and bust size. I would never weigh more than the Hollywood movie stars who were my height.

My mother had, for the duration of my teens, dragged me to every diet doctor in New York City. She was hoping for them to change me into the shape of a ballet dancer or supermodel. I was small, 5' 2", and lived by stuffing my face every two hours or so with doughnuts, candy, hamburgers, french fried onion rings, and pizza. If nothing else was available in the evenings after dinner when my parents went out to the movies, I ate Rice Krispies with chocolate sauce, after-dinner mints, and saltines by the box. I would eat whatever I could steal from the kitchen. I never experienced a full feeling, always searching for that one special food that would fill me and allow me to feel satisfied and stop eating. Night after night, I crawled into bed feeling gorged and guilty, reciting empty promises to begin dieting the next day. By the following evening, I was feeling the emptiness again and the cycle continued. I did not understand that the emptiness was inside my soul, not my stomach.

I lost thirty pounds in college by living on coffee, hard-boiled eggs, tuna, and apples, and with the aid of boxes and cartons of laxatives and cigarettes. I stayed small for decades. My greatest pleasure occurred the day my mother admired my figure in a size four skirt. I was, after all, a bulimic. No shame in that as long as I stayed small. What I enjoyed most was the memory of my pediatrician telling my mother during my adolescence, that I would lose the weight once I moved away from home.

For forty-five years I have counted every calorie that I consume, weighed myself every morning and periodically starved myself to reduce my size. When I quit smoking, my eating was more difficult to control and I resorted to using more laxatives and calorie counting. I began exercising at the gym every day, and was unable to miss a day of exercising without compensating by starving myself or indulging in laxatives. I live with constant shame and guilt. I constantly check my image in anything reflective to see if I am still in good shape, or if I have become flabby and fat since the last time I looked. I know it isn't logical, but I feel I have to check. I compare my body with every other woman I see, glorying if she exceeds me in size and weight, cursing her and myself if I exceed her. Two pounds too much and suicide seems preferable to this miserable obsession over food.

The preoccupation with food takes up more time in my brain than relationships, my work, children, and friends. I continue to prefer to eat alone or with equally food-obsessed people. I do not allow visitors to bring cakes, candy, or like foods into my house for fear I will binge eat all of it.

Recently, I have joined two support groups that have helped to begin balancing my life. I have stopped taking laxatives. I have joined a walking group to exercise for fun and health instead of my torture drills at the gym. Most importantly, I have learned to stop blaming my mother for not loving me enough so as a child I turned to food for comfort. I learn daily that what I eat or do not eat is entirely my responsibility.

Through my support groups, I have gained a deeper understanding about my eating disorder, and how to arrest it one day at a time. While I may never be cured of my bulimia, I have learned to fill my soul with healthier living, friends, family and work I truly enjoy, rather than the empty calories of my past.

ATTENTION DEFICIT DISORDER

Attention Deficit Disorder Test
Copyright, Michael Kunz, M.D. and Waguih William IsHak, M.D.
New York University Department of Psychiatry, 1996.

Answer the following questions Yes if they have been present since childhood.

1. Do you often have problems finishing tasks, or following through with projects?   _____

2. Is it hard for you to get organized?   _____

3. Is it hard for you to pay attention? Do you get easily distracted?   _____

4. Do you tend to "tune out" and daydream a lot?   _____

5. Do you have trouble starting tasks or projects? Do you put things off?   _____

6. Do you often make impulsive decisions? Do you often abruptly change your plans without thinking through the consequences?   _____

7. Do you often impulsively say things that make you unpopular, or that you later regret saying?   _____

8.   Do you suffer from frequent mood swings?   _____

9.   Do you often engage in thrill-seeking activities
      including the potentially dangerous ones?   _____

10.   Are you often impatient, irritable? Do you
      feel restless, edgy?   _____

11.   Do you easily get frustrated?   _____

12.   Do you talk a lot and often interrupt others?   _____

results

- -

The more you have answered **YES** to any of these questions,
the more serious your problem may be. Please consult with a
physician or licensed mental health professional experienced in
diagnosing and treating ADD.

- -

PERSONALITY DISORDERS

Screening for Personality Disorders

Copyright, Benjamin J. Sadock, M.D. and Waguih William IsHak, M.D. New York University Department of Psychiatry, 1996.

Answer Yes to the following questions ONLY if they have been present over a long period of time causing distress or impairment in functioning.

1. Do you suspect that others are exploiting, harming or deceiving you?   _____

2. Do you persistently bear grudges and not forget insults or injuries?   _____

3. Do you almost always choose solitary activities?   _____

4. Do you feel indifferent to praise or criticism of others?   _____

5. Do you experience recurrent strange day dreams or fantasies?   _____

6. Do you experience magical thinking that influences your behavior?   _____

7. Do you repeatedly get into conflicts
    with the law?   _____

8. Before age 18, have you been cruel to
    people or animals?   _____

9. Do you have a pattern of unstable and
    intense relationships with others?   _____

10. Do you have continuous feelings of emptiness?   _____

11. Do you feel uncomfortable in situations
    where you are not the center of attention?   _____

12. Are you easily influenced by others or
    are you suggestible?   _____

13. Are you generally envious of other people?   _____

14. Are you preoccupied with unlimited
    success or ideal love?   _____

15. Are you unwilling to get involved
    with people unless you are certain
    of being liked?   _____

16. Do you view yourself as socially inept,
    personally unappealing or inferior to others?   _____

17. Do you have a difficulty making everyday decisions without an excessive amount of advice and reassurance from others? _____

18. Are you preoccupied with fears of being left to take care of yourself? _____

19. Are you preoccupied with details, rules, lists, order, organization, or schedules? _____

20. Are you such a perfectionist that it interferes with your work? _____

results

The more you have answered **YES** to any of these questions, the more serious your problem may be. Please consult with a physician or licensed mental health professional experienced in diagnosing and treating personality disorders.

AL-ANON CODEPENDENCY QUESTIONS

From the Al-Anon Family Group Headquarters 20 Questions

1.   Do you constantly seek approval and affirmation?

2.   Do you fail to recognize your accomplishments?

3.   Do you fear criticism?

4.   Do you overextend yourself?

5.   Have you had problems with your own compulsive behavior?

6.   Do you have a need for perfection?

7.   Are you uneasy when your life is going smoothly, continually anticipating problems?

8.   Do you feel more alive in the midst of a crisis?

9.   Do you still feel responsible for others, as you did for the problem drinker in your life?

10.   Do you care for others easily, yet find it difficult to take care of yourself?

11.   Do you isolate yourself from other people?

12.   Do you respond with fear to authority figures and angry people?

13.   Do you feel that individuals and society in general are taking advantage of you?

14. Do you have trouble with intimate relationships?

15. Do you confuse pity with love, as you did with the problem drinker?

16. Do you attract and/or seek people who tend to be compulsive and/or abusive?

17. Do you cling to relationships because you are afraid of being alone?

18. Do you often mistrust your own feelings, and the feelings expressed by others?

19. Do you find it difficult to identify and express your emotions?

20. Do you think parental drinking may have affected you?

- -

Note: If there are mental illnesses or addictive behaviors in your family, you can ask yourself the same questions using those instead of problem drinking or other substance abuse or addiction.

- -

ALATEEN CODEPENDENCY QUESTIONS

From Al-Anon Family Group Headquarters 20 Questions for Teens

1. Do you have a parent, close friend or relative whose drinking upsets you?

2. Do you cover up your real feelings by pretending you don't care?

3. Are holidays and gatherings spoiled because of drinking?

4. Do you tell lies to cover up for someone else's drinking or what's happening in your home?

5. Do you stay out of the house as much as possible because you hate it there?

6. Are you afraid to upset someone for fear it will set off a drinking bout?

7. Do you feel nobody really loves you or cares what happens to you?

8. Are you afraid or embarrassed to bring your friends home?

9. Do you think the drinker's behavior is caused by you, other members of your family, friends, or rotten breaks in life?

10. Do you make promises about behavior, such as, "I'll get better school marks, go to church or keep my room clean" in exchange for a promise that the drinking and fighting stop?

11. Do you make threats such as, "If you don't stop drinking, fighting, I'll run away?"

12. Do you feel that if your mom or dad loved you, she or he would stop drinking?

13. Do you ever threaten or actually hurt yourself to scare your parents into saying, "I'm sorry," or "I love you"?

14. Do you believe no one could possibly understand how you feel?

15. Do you have money problems because of someone else's drinking?

16. Are mealtimes frequently delayed or disrupted because of the drinker?

17. Have you considered calling the police because of the drinkers' abusive behavior?

18. Have you refused dates out of fear or anxiety?

19. Do you think your problems would be solved if the drinking stopped?

20. Do you ever treat people (teachers, schoolmates, teammates, etc.) unjustly because you are angry at someone else for drinking too much?

- -

Note: If there are mental illnesses or addictive behaviors in your family, you can ask yourself the same questions using those instead of problem drinking or other substance abuse or addiction.

- -

SEX ADDICTION

Questions based on 10 signs Dr. Patrick Carnes identified as indicating sexual addiction in his book Don't Call It Love: Recovery from Sexual Addiction.

1.   Is your sexual behavior often out of your control?

2.   Have there been severe consequences due to your sexual behavior?

3.   Is there an inability to stop this high-risk behavior despite severe consequences?

4.   Do you keep on trying, or wanting to try, to stop or limit your sexual behavior?

5.   Do you use sex, sexual fantasy, porn in books, movies, on the Internet, as your primary way to relieve anxiety, to cope with emotions?

6.   Has your sexual activity increased because past levels were no longer enough to relieve anxiety?

7.   When you don't get enough sex, do you experience bad feelings that range from boredom to loneliness and isolation to depression?

8.   Do you spend most of your time getting sex, having sex, thinking about sex you have had or are going to have, or recovering from previous sexual experiences?

9.   Do you neglect school, work, friendships, family
     life, other kinds of fun and activity because of sexual
     behavior?

10. Is sex the driving force and interest in your life?

----

*Note: You can substitute 'romance' or 'falling in love, being in
love' for sex to discover if you are a romance addict.*

STORY

Just Tell Me You Love Me

Missy was small for her age and looked, with her huge eyes and the fair hair that drifted round her face, much younger than sixteen.

It was the night of the Homecoming Dance, and her friends persuaded Missy to go with their group.

"No boy will dance with me—they treat me like someone's little sister."

"Who cares? We'll all dance together."

Missy cared. She cared desperately that not one boy, ever, had asked her out or even spoken to her as if she were a girl, not just somebody else's friend.

"It'll be cool," her friends insisted as they all crammed into one of the school buses sent around town to pick up a high school full of students for Homecoming.

"It'll be even more cool with some of this inside you," said someone, passing a bottle back over the bus seat to Missy.

There were lots of bottles being passed around the darkened bus, and there was a lot of laughter.

When their bus pulled up in front of the school gym, Missy as well as her friends was ready to have fun. Music roared through the open doors to greet them.

The gym was dark, with fairy lights strung above their heads, and a spinning mirrored ball. Colors flashed behind the school band on the stage. There were adult chaperones around the gym's edges, but they seemed to fade into the walls and out of Missy's consciousness.

With sudden bravery, Missy allowed herself to be pulled onto the dance floor. She danced as long as she could pretend anybody cared and then as always she retreated into the shadows.

"Hey," a male someone said softly near her ear. An arm circled her waist. Missy couldn't believe how lovely it felt, even if the boy had made a mistake and it wasn't Missy he wanted.

"Hey yourself," she leaned against him to whisper.

"Can't hear a thing in here. Want to go for a walk?"

Missy let herself be led out into the cooling evening. She shivered, and the male arm was quick to shield her from the night air.

"You look good tonight," said Charlie, his breath soft in Missy's hair, as he led her farther away from the school grounds and down the road where the town's small cemetery had forever provided privacy to young couples.

It provided Missy with privacy that night of the Homecoming Dance.

"Just tell me you love me, Charlie," was all she asked.

Charlie loved Missy that night and for a few more nights in the following weeks.

One evening, though, when Charlie couldn't make their date, he sent his best friend Troy to take Missy to the movie he had promised.

"I know someplace better than a movie," Troy said, "Do you mind?"

He had borrowed his father's car, and he drove Missy to a café downtown by the water where the harbor lights shone on the docks and the fishing boats rocked gently in the moonlight and the music from the bar played softly in the darkness.

"They don't look too hard at I.D.'s here," said Troy, as they slipped into a dim booth. "What'll you have?"

Missy was feeling really anxious. Had Charlie told Troy they'd had sex? Charlie wouldn't. He loved her. He had said so.

But after a few drinks, Missy began to relax. She wasn't sure Troy wasn't just as attentive, just as attractive, as Charlie. Maybe even more so.

Troy drove them to a motel blinking neon lights near a gas station at the edge of town.

It was the first of an endless series of motel rooms for Missy, and all she ever asked for was,

"Just tell me you love me."

FOOD ADDICTION

These questions are taken from the Food Addicts in Recovery Anonymous web site:

1. Have you ever wanted to stop eating and found you just couldn't?

2. Do you think about food or your weight constantly?

3. Do you find yourself attempting one diet or food plan after another, with no lasting success?

4. Do you binge and then "get rid of the binge" through vomiting, exercise, laxatives, or other forms of purging?

5. Do you eat differently in private than you do in front of other people?

6. Has a doctor or family member ever approached you with concern about your eating habits or weight?

7. Do you eat large quantities of food at one time (binge)?

8. Is your weight problem due to your 'nibbling' all day long?

9. Do you eat to escape from your feelings?

10. Do you eat when you're not hungry?

11. Have you ever discarded food, only to retrieve and eat it later?

12. Do you eat in secret?

13.   Do you fast or severely restrict your food intake?

14.   Have you ever stolen other people's food?

15.   Have you ever hidden food to make sure you have 'enough'?

16.   Do you feel driven to exercise excessively to control your weight?

17.   Do you obsessively calculate the calories you've burned against the calories you've eaten?

18.   Do you frequently feel guilty or ashamed about what you've eaten?

19.   Are you waiting for your life to begin "when you lose the weight?"

20.   Do you feel hopeless about your relationship with food?

GAMBLING ADDICTION

Gamblers Anonymous offers these questions on which to decide whether you are a problem gambler.

1.   Did you ever lose time from work or school due to gambling?

2.   Has gambling ever made your home life unhappy?

3.   Did gambling affect your reputation?

4.   Have you ever felt remorse after gambling?

5.   Did you ever gamble to get money with which to pay debts or otherwise solve financial difficulties?

6.   Did gambling cause a decrease in your ambition or efficiency?

7.   After losing did you feel you must return as soon as possible and win back your losses?

8.   After a win did you have a strong urge to return and win more?

9.   Did you often gamble until your last dollar was gone?

10.   Did you ever borrow to finance your gambling?

11.   Have you ever sold anything to finance your gambling?

12.   Were you reluctant to use 'gambling money' for normal expenditures?

13.   Did gambling make you careless of the welfare of yourself or your family?

14.   Did you ever gamble longer than you had planned?

15.   Have you ever gambled to escape worry or trouble?

16.   Have you ever committed or considered committing, an illegal act to finance gambling?

17.   Did gambling cause you to have difficulty in sleeping?

18.   Do arguments, disappointments, or frustrations create within you an urge to gamble?

19.   Did you ever have an urge to celebrate any good fortune by a few hours of gambling?

20.   Have you ever considered self-destruction or suicide as a result of your gambling?

SHOPPING/SPENDING ADDICTION

The Illinois Institute for Addiction Recovery suggests these questions.

1.   Do you shop or spend money as a result of being disappointed, scared, or angry?

2.   Do shopping or spending habits cause you emotional distress or chaos in your life?

3.   Do you have arguments with others regarding your shopping or spending habits?

4.   Do you have frequent arguments in your own head about your shopping or spending habits?

5. Do you feel lost without credit cards, or ways of getting credit?

6. Do you buy items on credit you wouldn't buy with cash?

7. Does spending money give you a rush or a high and anxiety at the same time?

8. Do spending and shopping feel like reckless or forbidden acts?

9. Do you feel guilty, ashamed, embarrassed, or confused after shopping or spending money?

10. Do you buy things you never use?

11. Do you lie to others about what you bought or how much money you spent?

12. Do you think excessively about money?

13. Do you spend a lot of time counting your money and juggling what you owe to be able to shop and spend money?

STORY He Gambled His Life

believe it started out innocently enough. At seven years of age, I would join in neighborhood games with the other boys; flipping baseball cards, pitching pennies, knocking bottle tops or marbles out of the ring. Each of us "gambling" that our effort would result in a win and the accumulation of everyone else's cards or tops. It wasn't until my twelfth year that my church introduced a carnival wheel during one of its fund-raising fairs. For a quarter, I could "guess" what color or number the ball would land on after the wheel stopped spinning. There was nothing wrong with my betting on the outcome of the wheel's spin. After all, the church to which my family belonged was hosting the fair. While my friends enjoyed the rides and games at the fair, I remained planted at the wheel for the duration of the carnival. Before going to the carnival, I planned to stop playing at the wheel when I was ahead in quarters. I never stopped until I ran out of money. It was the same experience every year when I went to the carnival.

Ever since I can remember, my family and others around me gambled. They bet and they drank alcohol. My mother played bingo at our church. At first, just on Saturdays. Then, she found other churches that hosted bingo on the other nights. Her schedule of bingo was so regular, the family became accustomed to having my mother spend her evenings at "church".

I was intensely attracted to the excitement of gambling. The fantasy of predicting and controlling the outcome. I felt nervous most of the time, and gambling served as an outlet; a release from all the pent up anxiety and energy. As my drive to gamble increased, my need to wager more in order to achieve the same thrill increased. Quarters turned into dollars, which evolved into bets larger than I could cover. I became enraged when I lost and determined to regain control of the betting and the outcome. I discovered that drinking alcohol took the edge off my anxiety and helped me reach the level of excitement I craved.

My drinking unleashed an uninhibited, rage-filled addict. I was unaffected by good sense or judgment. At age thirteen I was drunk and accepted a dare to drive my girlfriend's parents' car. I made it as far as the oak tree on her family's front lawn. It took the "jaws of life" to remove me from the car and a surgeon to remove the rearview mirror from the right side of my forehead.

Unaffected by that experience, I continued to take bets and drink. I couldn't stop. I felt it was the only way to medicate the anxiety and release the charge for excitement. I played bingo, bet on college and pro sports, and even the "scratch off" ticket games. As the gambling losses accumulated, so did my rage. The control I convinced myself I had was quickly slipping away. I wanted to take my frustration out with my hands. I was frightened of the amount I was gambling and losing, and anxious that my superstitious rituals were not successfully controlling the outcome of my playing. I was rage in motion, waiting for a match to combust.

I combusted during a poker game at my parents' home. After several rounds of my best friend taunting my losses, I saw red. I lunged for him with all my energy, anxiety, and fear. It took several friends and my father to pry my hands off his neck. This experience should have shown me how life threatening my addictions to gambling and drinking were. I would have killed him.

I graduated from high school because I was the captain of the basketball, baseball, and soccer teams, and they passed me on. I worked after graduating to support my gambling and drinking. The gambling debts became too expensive and I needed to borrow from my family in order to keep the bookies at a safe distance. Each time I came to my family I would swear to them and myself that this was the end of it. I would control my drinking and gambling. Some mornings during the painful withdrawal from alcohol, I would swear to myself and God that I would quit. But, by nightfall I was at it again; hustling to get the money to cover a bet or play at the casinos, and drinking. When I lost, my rage would surface and I frequently ended up my night in an emergency room or dark alley, nursing my wounds, uttering more empty promises to myself about quitting. Sometimes, I hoped the fights I got into would result in my death. While I feared dying, I was also afraid to live. Many nights I contemplated suicide. My drinking and gambling resulted in my losing job after job and then my home. Homeless and penniless, I stayed at those friends' homes who allowed me to sleep on their couches for a night. Sometimes I slept in the park. I was cold, hungry, and desperately afraid, not knowing how to interrupt this path of self-destruction.

I discovered the name for my addictive disease during treatment in a thirty-day alcohol rehabilitation center after being picked up by the police for vagrancy. I was twenty-six years old.

When I was released from the rehabilitation program, I began attending twelve-step programs for both alcohol and gambling. The self-help meetings provided me with the cognitive and psychological tools to learn how to live life on life's terms. I was able to handle my fears without escaping into drinking or gambling. I acquired mentors, also called sponsors, in each program, who helped me to apply the principles of the twelve steps to different situations that would arise in my life. It is in large part due to my sponsors that I was able to recover my sense of peace and connection to the community in which I now live. I was given a second chance at living eighteen years ago.

During the course of my recovery, I completed training as a mortician and obtained a position in a funeral home. One of my duties was to respond to calls from morgues, hospitals, and family homes to pick up and to deliver the body to the funeral home for embalming and other preparatory work. On one occasion, a pick up call resulted in my going to the city morgue.

When I arrived, I looked at the toe tag with astonishment. The dead man was my gambling sponsor who had a severe gambling relapse and effectively ended his own life. His last message to me was clear: I gambled my life. I lost.

I have carried his message every day into my life. I have not cured my anxiety or depression, although I have techniques to help me when I feel nervous. While I have had a few gambling relapses over the years, I seek help from the people in my twelve-step group. My sponsor's message reminds me that I am given each day to renew my commitment to my life and to the rejuvenated relationships I have with my family and friends.

SECTION THREE

Addiction Dictionary

The definitions in this section are based on many of the books listed in the Bibliography, particularly:

- *The American Psychiatric Association's Diagnostic and Statistical Manual of Mental Disorders* (4th ed.), DSMIV
- *U.S. News & World Report*
- *Addiction: Why Can't They Just Stop?*
- *The Courage to Lead: Mental Illnesses & Addictions*
- *Living with Disabilities*
- *The Teen Brain Book: Who and What Are You?*
- *Are You Human, or What? Evolutionary Psychology*

The point of this addiction dictionary is:

- To provide further explanations of terms related to addiction and recovery.
- To supplement information in previous chapters.
- To stand on its own as a dictionary for the field of addiction and recovery.

A

- -

abuse Repeated, excessive use of harmful substances, alcohol, drugs, nicotine, inhalants, or repeated, excessive repetition of harmful behaviors such as gambling, binge-eating, compulsive shopping, sexual acting-out. Abusive use of substances and abusive behaviors not only often escalate into addictions, but can cause immediate harm: sexually transmitted diseases (STDs), AIDS; brain damage, insanity, death, arrest leading to jail time, car accidents, physical injury, manslaughter.

addiction Physical, emotional, mental craving for particular substances or behaviors, increasing tolerance that demands more and more to get high, the pain of withdrawal symptoms, and continued use despite adverse consequences.

Alcoholics Anonymous World-wide support groups founded in 1935 by Bill Wilson, an alcoholic himself who discovered that the best help for an alcoholic was the support of other alcoholics who understood both the active addiction and how to stop drinking and stay stopped. He wrote *Alcoholics Anonymous* and *Twelve Steps and Twelve Traditions* of recovery from active alcoholism, and founded Alcoholics Anonymous, a worldwide network of groups for which there are no dues or fees, whose only requirement for membership is the desire to stop drinking. See offshoot support groups: Al-Anon (for families and friends of alcoholics); Alateen (for teen recovery, teens at risk); Association for Children of Alcoholics; National Council on Alcoholism and Drug Dependence; National

Institute on Alcohol Abuse and Alcoholism; Narcotics Anonymous and more. *See Help Resources, page 182.*

alcoholism Progressive physical and mental disease that becomes worse over time. Symptoms include increasingly heavy drinking despite consequences: physical danger; legal jeopardy (arrests, car accidents); relationship, family, school, work problems; mood swings, personality changes, anxiety, headaches, nausea; difficulty in controlling amount, when to stop. In later stages, indications include increased tolerance, inability to cut down, blackout drinking, tremors, seizures, hallucinations, and other withdrawal symptoms. *See self-test, page 105.* Causes: Research suggests about 50% genetic brain chemistry; 50% environment, stress, emotional and behavioral disorders, mental illness.

amphetamines See drugs.

anorexia nervosa Severe eating disorder: symptoms include an intense preoccupation with food and a fear of gaining weight. People with this disorder both limit food intake and binge-eat, then obsessed with overeating, often purge with laxatives or by vomiting, take diet pills, push food around plate instead of eating. Body weight is low for height, anorexics feel fat even when thin. Starvation to the point of death is possible without treatment. *See self-test, page 113.* Causes: family and cultural beliefs about body size, brain chemistry, co-occurring psychiatric disorders, control issues. See bulimia, obsessive-compulsive disorder.

anxiety disorders Emotional disorders and illnesses often overwhelming, often progressive, often leading to substance addiction or addictive behaviors to obtain relief.

Generalized Anxiety Disorder (GAD): Excessive concerns over money, health, family, work. Physical symptoms may include trembling, headaches, irritability, sweating, nausea, difficulty in concentrating.

Panic Disorder: Repeated episodes of intense fear accompanied by physical symptoms such as chest pain, breathing difficulty, dizziness.

Agoraphobia: Fear for safety, of open spaces, fear of situations and places from which it is thought escape could be embarrassing or difficult. Physical symptoms are similar to panic attacks.

Social Phobia: Fear of being looked at in social situations, persistent performance anxiety, avoidance of people, places, activities that might expose the sufferer to shame. Physical symptoms include palpitations, sweating, trembling.

Also see: PTSD, OCD.

Studies show that teens with anxiety disorders are at greater risk for turning to smoking, drinking alcohol, using drugs, gambling, compulsive shopping, sex, overeating, and other compulsive-obsessive behaviors for relief.

attention deficit hyperactivity disorder (ADHD) Developmental disorder characterized by disorganized thinking, impulsiveness and problems in self-control, difficulty in completing tasks, forgetfulness, procrastination, inattention unless extremely passionate about a particular activity for which everything else may be sacrificed. Boys have the hyperactivity component more often than girls. Teens with these problems may be at risk for alcohol and drug abuse to ease their chronic anxiety.

B

---

binging In terms of substance or behavior addictions, periodic rather than daily excessive, compulsive, unrestrained indulgence in substances like alcohol or drugs or in behaviors like eating, gambling, buying; may be symptomatic of full-blown disease of alcoholism or addiction; may be symptomatic of co-occurring mental disorders.

bipolar disorder Mood disorder (manic-depression) in which moods swing from manic (inflated self-esteem, hyperactive, unrestrained, hyperenergetic, impulsive activity, little need to sleep) to depressed (distinct drop in mood, often worst at waking and during late afternoon); daily loss of energy, either sleeping too much or cannot sleep; unplanned loss or increase of appetite; physical lethargy; disinterest even in favorite activities; difficulty in concentrating or even caring; movements are in slow motion or display agitation; feelings are of deep sadness, even escalating to thoughts or plans of suicide; there is morbid self-centeredness, preoccupation with guilt, worthlessness.

blackouts Total memory loss for minutes, hours, even days, are one result of drug and alcohol abuse, a form of drug-induced brain damage in which the electrical storm caused by the drugs fouls up communication lines and memory storage in the brain.

body dysmorphic disorder BDD is an excessive concern with body image, imagined abnormalities or defects; this may result in overuse of dieting, plastic surgery, beauty supplies to correct perceived flaws in hair, skin, face, muscles, wrinkles, nose shape, breast size, buttocks, genitals; rituals involve constant self-preoccupation and examination; BBD is an unrealistic body perception no surgery or cosmetic ever addresses or corrects.

bulimia nervosa An eating disorder defined as periods of binge-eating in which large quantities of food are eaten, and then purged (vomiting, laxatives, diuretics) or through excessive exercise. Food is used addictively as a reward or to ward off anxiety, to comfort, to escape reality. Bulimics eat too fast and too much; they prefer to eat alone to hide quantity; guilt, self-hate, depression occur after binging. *See self-test, page 113.*

C

caffeine A stimulant primarily used in the form of coffee, tea, and soft drinks that acts on the central nervous system: 8 oz. coffee contains about 125 mg of caffeine, tea has 60 mg, soft drink 40 mg, although there are products now with mega amounts of caffeine. Studies show that more than 250 mg causes irritability, restlessness, sleeplessness, anxiety. Tolerance can be developed for caffeine, so more is needed for the same jolt.

club drugs Drugs such as Ecstasy. Rohypnol, Ketamine and other date-rape drugs can cause memory loss, brain damage, and death, according to the National Institute on Drug Abuse.

cocaine, crack cocaine See drugs.

codependency In *Codependent No More*, Melody Beattie defines a codependent as "anyone who has let another person's behavior affect him or her, and who is obsessed with controlling that person's behavior." Person addiction includes a fear of being alone or abandoned, a need to be needed so intense that mates and friends are usually chosen among other dependent or addicted personalities. *See self-test, page 126.*

co-occurring disorders Mental illnesses, psychiatric problems: a brain hijacked by drugs usually has an increased possibility of previous and ongoing anxiety disorder, depression, PTSD, learning disabilities, schizophrenia, ADHD. Addiction treatment must include treating the mental disorder or relapse will likely occur.

cosmetic surgery addiction An addiction to repeated surgeries on face and body to correct usually imaginary defects based on a cultural ideal often called perfectionism, but more accurately on BDD (body dysmorphic disorder) or OCD (obsessive compulsive disorder) .

cough syrup Over-the-counter or prescription cough medication often contains addictive substances like codeine and alcohol. Abuse of certain cough syrups like Robotussin can induce hallucinations and death.

cutting An addiction to self-inflicted physical pain sometimes for attention, usually to relieve intense psychological anguish: knife, scissors, razor, whatever is available is used on stomach (where it won't show), arms, legs, face where it will show.

cybersex addiction (Internet, TV pornography) Release from anxiety, depression, loneliness, like any other drug or addictive behavior, with the added component of intimacy fears, possible social or environmental phobias.

D

- -

date rape Forced sexual assault by a person known to the victim, most usually perpetrated on adolescent females, but even on adolescent males, by males.

denial Psychological mechanism, often unconscious, used by alcoholics/ addicts, to minimize accusations of abuse in order to protect their habit; friends and families of alcoholics/addicts also use the mechanism to avoid facing and dealing with the problem.

dependence More severe condition than abuse; medical professionals will look for physical symptoms such as: 1) tolerance (when a person needs more of a drug to achieve the desired effect or to ward off withdrawal symptoms) and 2) withdrawal symptoms when drug use is reduced or stopped. Professionals also look for behavioral criteria such as 1) being unable to stop once using starts, 2) avoidance of responsibilities, work, school, social activities to spend more time using; 3) continued use despite personality, health, and relationship deterioration.

depression Major depression is a mood disorder the symptoms of which are a severe drop in mood, a loss of interest and pleasure in life: the profound sadness and loss of joy and energy are not situational but physiological, neurochemical, genetic in origin. See also manic-depression or bipolar disorder.

detoxification The first stage, but not the only stage, of treatment for alcoholism and drug addiction, is to cleanse, deprive the system of the toxic substance: sometimes rest is enough, but after prolonged and heavy use of alcohol, opiates, tranquilizers, supervised medical treatment of withdrawal symptoms reduces the severity, pain, craving. After stabilization, life changes and continued treatment and rehabilitation are necessary, just as for any other progressive disease such as diabetes.

drugs The included drugs and alcohol list (page 160-163) and its schedule of effects, risks, and withdrawal symptoms is partial. Further numbers and addresses for help are listed in an appendix at the back of this book. Also, see *A Teen's Guide to Living Drug-Free* by Bettie B. Youngs and Jennifer Leigh Youngs.

dual diagnosis Presence of one or more psychiatric disorders as well as alcoholism or drug addiction, such as depression, anxiety disorder, schizophrenia, bipolar disorder, OCD, or one of the other behavioral addictions.

- -

eating disorders See anorexia, bulimia.

Ecstasy See drugs.

DRUGS AND ALCOHOL

	Effects	Risks	Withdrawal
Depressants			
ALCOHOL Beer, Wine, Hard Liquor	distortion of reality impaired coordination exaggerated emotions impaired judgment slurred speech, aggression	blackouts sex drive loss brain damage death	insomnia anxiety seizures DT's (delirium tremens) fatality, strokes possible
BARBITURATES Nembutal, Phenobarbital	bloodshot eyes argumentativeness confusion, dizziness	brain damage coma, death	convulsions, nausea cramps, delirium fatality, strokes possible
TRANQUILIZERS Ativan, BZD, Klonopin, Librium, Valium, Xanax	confusion sleepiness detachment	heart problems, chronic anxiety, overdose, death	agitation, cramps, nausea, tremors fatality, strokes possible
Stimulants			
COCAINE Crack (smoked cocaine)	excessive activity and talk, agitation, belligerence, dilated pupils	brain seizures, 'bugs crawling on skin,' insomnia, violence, paranoia, head & stomach aches, depression	pain, cravings, delusions

AMPHETAMINES METHAMPHETAMINES Crank (Street name)	same and more	same plus tics, convulsions	delirium, suicidal thoughts
RITALIN	agitation, anxiety talkativeness	anxiety, insomnia, irritability	fatigue, headaches
CAFFEINE (Tea, Coffee, Energy Drinks)	increased heart rate, activity, and talk	gastric pains, ulcers anxiety, insomnia, jittery nerves	headaches fatigue irritability
NICOTINE (cigarettes, cigars,) pipe tobacco, snuff	increased blood pressure and heart rate, reduced appetite	cancer, heart and lung disease, stroke, breathing problems	aggression intense craving depression concentration problems
Opiates/Narcotics			
HEROIN MORPHINE OPIUM PRESCRIPTION PAINKILLERS*	apathy, constricted pupils slowed breathing, possible needle marks, impaired thinking, high risk of illness, stupor	collapsed veins, impotence, coma, overdose, death	pain nausea cramps chills intense cravings

*Vicodin, oxycodone, OxyContin, Percocet, Percodan

DRUGS AND ALCOHOL

	Effects	Risks	Withdrawal
Inhalants			
CONSUMER AEROSOLS, FREON PAINT, NAIL POLISH REMOVERS, AIRPLANE GLUE, CLEANING SOLVENTS	irrational behavior, runny nose, drowsiness, slurred speech, distortion of reality	brain damage coma, death asphyxiation hallucinations	confusion headache
DEPRESSIVE INHALANTS Amyl nitrate Butyl nitrate	above, plus flushed face, neck	blood vessel damage, heart attack	
Cannabinoids			
MARIJUANA	craving for sweets less inhibited red eyes forgetfulness	memory loss lethargy psychosis	anxiety fatigue despair
HASHISH	same, plus distorted senses, inability to think clearly	same, plus impotence, loss of reasoning ability	same, plus anorexia insomnia

Hallucinogens, Club Or Designer Drugs: Psychedelics

LSD (ACID)	sensory distortion, hallucinations, insomnia, mood swings, violence, time loss, dilated pupils	bad trips, catatonia, schizoid behavior, coma, convulsions, permanent loss of reality	flashbacks, insomnia
MDMA (ECSTASY)	confusion, insomnia, distorted reality, accelerated heart rate, hallucinations	brain damage, convulsions, death	insomnia, irritability

Note: With LSD, MDMA, as well as marijuana, you don't know what extra dangerous chemicals or in what possibly fatal doses dealers have mixed with the drug.

KETAMINE	delusions, dissociation, babbling, bad taste	amnesia, delirium, death	anxiety, depression
ROHYPNOL (Date Rape Drug)	confusion, sleepiness	blackouts, confusion, date rape, death	agitation, tremors, cramps
PCP (Angel Dust)	delusions, self-destructive behavior, unnatural stare, violence	flashbacks, suicidal anxiety, confusion, isolation	cravings, depression, insomnia, tremors

enabler A person who excuses, who rescues, who interferes with another's behavior in such a way as to protect her or him from the harmful consequences of that behavior. Enabling describes the behavior of friends and families of addicts/alcoholics when they call in sick, cover for them, explain away drugged or drunk behavior, or in the case of addictive behaviors like compulsive shopping, pay their debts. Enablers often have a hard time understanding that covering up the addiction only prolongs it.

euphoria That advanced state of mental and emotional bliss and freedom from any anxiety all alcoholics/addicts try to reach, whether through alcohol, drugs, gambling, sex, food, extreme exercise, whatever the mood altering drug or behavior of choice.

exercise addiction Not yet recognized as a clinical disorder by the American Psychiatric Association. But in our weight-and-fitness-obsessed society, exercise addicts exercise obsessively. Increased amounts of exercise become necessary, even to the point of injury, loss of relationship, and work time, to achieve the required high. Anxiety and other withdrawal symptoms are experienced when exercise time is curtailed.

extreme sports dependence Obsessive-compulsive need to engage in life-threatening sports such as race-car-driving, bungee-jumping, sky-diving, hang-gliding, dangerous mountain-or-rock-climbing for the thrill that brings an adrenaline rush to the brain. See risk behavior addiction.

F

fame See popularity, self-importance as addictions.

food addiction See anorexia nervosa, bulimia nervosa.

G

gambling Pathologically addicted, compulsive gamblers are not social gamblers. They are preoccupied with the high, the desired excitement of spending money to make more money. They obsess over past, present, and future gambling. They continue to gamble even to the financial deprivation of family and friends. Irrational systems and rituals based on the gambler's beliefs in her or his ability to control outcomes often accompany the winning and losing of bets. *See self-test, page 139.*

gossip An addiction to verbal violence in people who compulsively put down other people in order to feel good about thinking themselves "in."

H

hallucinations See drugs.

hallucinogens See drugs.

hangover Short-term effect of drinking too much alcohol can include pounding headache, shakes, nausea, insomnia, inner trembling.

hashish See drugs.

heroin See drugs.

I

----

impulse control disorders and addictions See obsessive compulsive disorder (OCD), pathological gambling, compulsive shopping, body dysmorphic disorder (BDD), eating disorders, alcohol and drug addictions, kleptomania: also on the list of impulse control disorders are trichotillomania (pulling out hair compulsively from any part of the body); hypochondria (fear derived from imagining signs of medical illness despite being healthy); and Tourette's Disorder (uncontrollable sudden rapid movements, words, or sounds) .

Internet addiction disorder Cyberpsychologists, according to *U.S. News & World Report*, define IAD as a preoccupation with a virtual world that substitutes for the real world, interfering with real relationships, studies, work, friends, and family. When deprived of their Internet time, those with IAD grow anxious or depressed as in withdrawal from any other addiction. Also destructive in Internet addiction is the availability of drugs, porn, internet sex, gambling, and the chat rooms also accessible to perverts preying on the innocent.

J

junk food See overeating.

K

Ketamine See drugs.

kleptomania Repeated and compulsive stealing for excitement, psychological reward, or to relieve anxiety: this disorder is distinguished from shoplifting which is based on personal gain.

L

LSD See drugs.

love Affection, passion with no dependency, no attachment, no need.

M

major depression Loss of interest and pleasure in life, a deep sadness and fatigue, based not in external situations but in one's own brain chemistry.

manic depression Mood swings from manic (inflated self-esteem, grandiosity, hyperactive, unrestrained behavior, little need to sleep, impulsive activity like falling in or out of love, compulsive shopping sprees, sudden traveling) to depressive (see major depression symptoms). Unpredictable, frightening mood disorder of the brain chemistry, not based on external situations.

marijuana See drugs.

mental illness Like any other physical illness, the loss of the ability to function, to think and behave appropriately in daily life; the inability of the brain to accurately identify and process experiences, to respond or adapt effectively to the ordinary world, to relationships, to the activities in our human environment.

methadone Synthetically made narcotic used to treat opiate addiction such as heroin and oxycodone. Also used recreationally and for chronic pain management. Withdrawal can be as severe as from heroin.

methamphetamine Synthetically made narcotic.

mood State of emotional being such as sadness, happiness, fear (boredom and anxiety are low-grade states of fear) .

mood disorders See depression, manic-depression (bipolar disorder), anxiety disorder.

morphine See drugs.

mushrooms See drugs, hallucinogens.

N

narcotics Opioid-based drugs, legal and illegal, prescription, club, and street. The United States DEA (Drug Enforcement Administrations) has imposed the Controlled Substances Act with schedules (lists) of those drugs used for medical purposes such as OxyContin and those drugs for which there is no current medical use such as heroin.

Narcotics Anonymous A program for those addicted to drugs based on the 12 Step Program of Alcoholics Anonymous. *See Help Resources, page 182.*

nicotine See drugs.

Nicotine Anonymous A program for those addicted to nicotine based on the 12 Step Program of Alcoholics Anonymous. *See Help Resources, page 182.*

O

obsessive-compulsive disorder (OCD) A form of anxiety disorder; people with OCD suffer from recurrent, persistent, unwanted, unrealistic thoughts and obsessions; ritualistic, unnecessary, and obsessive behaviors like counting and placing objects in a certain order; constant washing of hands, checking and rechecking lights, locks, the stove. The thoughts are the obsessions; the behaviors are the compulsions to overcome irrational, obsessive fears. *See Help Resources, page 182*, Anxiety Disorders Association of America, National Institute of Mental Health (NIMH).

overeating Eating more than is appropriate for height and body frame, resulting in obesity; this may be the result of food addiction, anxiety disorder, eating disorder, glandular imbalance, gene pool factors, developmental delays, the constant availability of inexpensive, supersized junk food, our sedentary lives.

over-the-counter medications Health drugs that do not require a prescription such as cold medications, cough syrups, pain killers, laxatives—all can be used and abused and turned into addictions.

Oxycodone See drugs.

PCP See drugs, hallucinogens.

people addiction See popularity addiction.

personality disorders Faulty perception of oneself and one's relationship with others, leading to unfulfilled expectations:

inflexible inability to perceive disordered self makes it difficult to change. Several personality disorders may coexist: borderline personality disorder symptoms, based on fear of abandonment, include unstable fluctuations between neediness and hypercritical rejection, inflation of self and excessive criticism; obsessive-compulsive personality disorder symptoms are a preoccupation with perfectionism (living up to conditioned standards), workaholism, and the need to control others.

popularity addiction What originated as an evolutionary imperative for a pack animal like humans—survival depends on acceptance by the group for food and protection—is exaggerated into an obsessive, dependent need for everyone's good opinion and constant approval.

possessions addiction An addiction to one's stuff, and to the acquisition of more stuff as a form of security; sometimes accompanied by an inability to throw anything away, sometimes referred to as pack-ratting or hoarding.

post-traumatic stress disorder (PTSD) Severe anxiety reaction to the shock of past painful events such as physical abuse, drug experiences, violence in families, on the streets, in war: PTSD often results in drug abuse to alleviate the psychological pain and flashbacks.

prescription drug abuse Unauthorized use of prescribed drugs.

prostitution addiction Teen boys and girls, especially runaways, as well as adults, exchange sex for money, often for drugs, and then become addicted to selling sex; this is especially possible for those who have suffered early childhood sexual abuse.

R

recovery Ending the use of addictive chemical substances and addictive behaviors involving the rewiring of brain circuits altered by drugs, alcohol, and maladaptive behaviors through treatment such as therapy, 12-step programs, medication or any combination of these.

rehabilitation Recovery from addiction, through institution, 12-step program, therapy, medication or all of the above.

relapse People trying to recover from addiction are doing so with brains altered by alcohol and drug and behavioral abuse, including diminished impulse control and strong cravings; the occasional return to former abuse is part of the disease as the brain is being rewired.

risk behavior addiction The rush of the brain's own adrenalin and other neurochemicals is experienced as a high in dangerous behaviors such as high risk mountain climbing, sky diving, motorcycle riding; addicts crave the high produced by their own neurochemistry in the face of danger.

Rohypnol Date-rape drug. See drugs.

romance addiction The high is the neurophysiological chemistry of being in love, the mental and emotional attraction that includes the excitement of meeting emotional, sexual, and mental needs, rescue needs, mutual dependencies, the need for exclusivity and the immature need for possession of another human being. Fear of loss heightens the above mixture of excitement, as does fear of discovery. May co-occur with, but is not identical to, sex addiction, the need for the high of constant sexual stimulation, sometimes with the same partner, often with a compulsion for a constant change of sexual partners, even of strangers. See sex addiction.

S

scheduled drugs The Drug Enforcement Administration (DEA) lists legal and illegal drugs according to their potential for addiction; a partial list includes:

Schedule I drugs are illegal, with the most potential for addiction: heroin, marijuana, Ecstasy.

Schedule II drugs, also with potential for abuse, are considered to have medical use, such as morphine, oxycodone, cocaine.

Schedule III drugs include some barbiturates, steroids, ketamine.

Schedule IV drugs include anti-anxiety drugs and sedatives like Xanax, Librium, Klonopin.

Schedule V drugs are over-the-counter preparations like cough and cold medicines.

schizophrenia Psychotic disturbance that may include a loss of contact with reality, the experience of delusions and hallucinations, inner-directed behaviors that may seem purposeless and unconnected to the outside environment, including repetitive, obsessive-compulsive, ritualistic behaviors.

security addiction Addictive, ritualistic behaviors that are supposed to protect physically and/or psychologically, whether that behavior is repetitive checking of locks on doors and windows or chronic co-dependency on other people or groups (tribalism or nationalism is a form of psychological security addiction) .

self-addiction Rigid clinging to one's own ideas, opinions, habits, one's own importance.

self-injury, self-mutilation Injuring oneself by making cuts or scratches on one's own body with an object sharp enough to break the skin and make it bleed, or burn the skin with the end of a lighted cigarette or match, evidenced by scars or marks on the body, often on the belly or legs and thus hidden by clothing: a desperate way of coping with terrible emotions or a bad situation, feelings too difficult to bear such as rage, sorrow, rejection, terror, emptiness, through the distraction of immediate physical pain: cutting often co-occurs with depression, obsessive thinking, other compulsive behaviors.

sex addiction Progressive disease like alcoholism and drug dependency in which the addict requires more and more of the high released by chemical/sexual hormones to satisfy the body's cravings: healthy relationships to other people, work, school, everything is sacrificed to temporary sexual pleasure, and this is accompanied by guilt, shame, fear of discovery of the out-of-control behavior, whether this occurs with people, or online with cybersex or pornography: compulsion to obsess about or to engage in frequent sexual activity regardless of health, legality, or other obligations and relationships: compulsive sex addicts are often unable to achieve emotional intimacy. *See self-test, page 130.* See Sex Addicts Anonymous.

shoplifting Stealing for personal gain, the paying of debts, to support the self and solve money issues instead of working for a living. The issues are different from the addictive behavior used for a thrill, a high, a 'rush.' See Kleptomania. See CASA (Cleptomania and Shoplifters Anonymous).

shopping/spending behavior addiction Chronic, repetitive compulsion to buy things and services often beyond the purchaser's means that gives the spender a temporary high followed by guilt, fear, shame at out-of-control debt as well as behavior: an impulse control disorder, similar to other addictive behavioral disorders. *See self-test, page 141.* See Debtor's Anonymous, Shopaholics Anonymous.

smoking Breathing in the addictive drugs nicotine, hashish, marijuana and other tobacco products through cigarettes, cigars, pipes. Chewing tobacco and inhaling snuff can also be addictive and dangerous to the health. See drugs.

substance abuse Repeated use of alcohol or other drugs, less severe than addiction in that the tolerance that requires increasingly greater quantities has not developed, but that still interferes with school, work, relationships, obligations.

suicide The killing, or attempted killing of oneself, a compulsion that often accompanies alcoholism, addiction to heroin or other drugs that impair judgment, and other psychiatric disorders such as bipolar disorder, depression, schizophrenia.

T

---

television addiction Compulsive dependency on watching television, not necessarily based on content but to escape life and its anxieties, as a substitute for real relationships with friends and family, as a passive distraction, to alleviate depression and its derivative boredom, as a mood-changer: *Scientific American* reports 3 hours a day for an average viewer, as much as 60 hours per week for television addicts.

tolerance A major symptom of addiction, in that increased amounts of alcohol and drugs are required to achieve the same high over time.

treatment Aided, supported recovery from substance and/or behavior addiction through outpatient programs such as Alcoholics Anonymous, Narcotics Anonymous, Debtors Anonymous, Sex Addicts Anonymous, or through short-term or long-term inpatient and outpatient rehabilitation facilities—or any combination of the above.

Twelve Steps of Alcoholics Anonymous The twelve-step programs are based on the original model created by Bill W. and Dr. Bob in order to help alcoholics stop drinking and recover their lives and relationships. Members come together to "share their experience, strength, and hope with each other that they may solve their common problem and help others to recover from alcoholism" as it states in the Preamble of Alcoholics Anonymous. The meetings can be open to anyone interested in learning about the recovery from alcoholism or closed, for alcoholics only. To be a member, one is only required to have a desire to stop drinking. The formats vary to include speaker, discussion, step, and beginner, meetings. While each meeting uses different materials, the dialogues often include spiritual and pragmatic topics such as gratitude, fear, willingness, anger, honesty, attitude, tolerance, humility, making amends, principles vs. personalities, resentments, and acceptance.

Other twelve-step programs have been modeled after the A.A. program such as Al-anon (for family and friends of those with an alcohol problem), Alateen (children of alcoholics), Overeaters Anonymous, Gamblers Anonymous, to name a few. The topics focused on in A.A. twelve-step meetings can be universally applied to all human beings interested in exploring the human condition, with or without alcohol addiction. (See p. 178-180)

U

----

uppers (amphetamines) See drugs.

TWELVE STEPS OF ALCOHOLICS ANONYMOUS

1. We admitted we were powerless over alcohol—that our lives had become unmanageable.

2. Came to believe that a Power greater than ourselves could restore us to sanity.

3. Made a decision to turn our will and our lives over the care of God as we understood Him.

4. Made a searching and fearless moral inventory of ourselves.

5. Admitted to God, to ourselves and to another human being the exact nature of our wrongs.

6. Were entirely ready to have God remove all these defects of character.

7. Humbly asked Him to remove our shortcomings.

8. Made a list of all persons we had harmed, and became willing to make amends to them all.

9. Made direct amends to such people wherever possible, except when to do so would injure them or others.

10. Continued to take personal inventory and when we were wrong promptly admitted it.

11. Sought through prayer and meditation to improve our conscious contact with God, as we understood Him, praying only for knowledge of His will for us and the power to carry that out.

12. Having had a spiritual awakening as the result of these steps, we tried to carry this message to alcoholics, and to practice these principles in all our affairs.

Valium See drugs.

Vicodin See drugs.

violence addiction A compulsive craving for the rush received from either witnessing or participating in brutality on animals or human beings: beatings, rape, torture, all the way up to murder.

----

withdrawal The physical and emotional/psychological symptoms, always uncomfortable, sometimes painful, experienced by an addict deprived of the substance, activity, person, place, or thing to which or on which a dependency has been formed: these range from severe physical and psychological symptoms in drug and alcohol withdrawal, biochemical trauma after death or abandonment in dependent relationships, severe depression when ending addictions to gambling, shopping, eating disorders, smoking to milder symptoms of anxiety, anger, and other emotional difficulties.

workaholism A behavioral addiction to the high of perceived self-importance, status, competence, orderliness, cultural virtue, drama, self-sacrifice conferred by overwork, often accompanied by fears or incompetence in personal relationships: as with any other addiction, work provides a high that other activities do not match, and withdrawal brings agitation, boredom, even depression.

HELP RESOURCES, ORGANIZATIONS, WEBSITES

Al-Anon
1600 Corporate Landing
  Parkway
Virginia Beach, VA 23454
(757) 563-1600
www.al-anon.org

**Alcoholics Anonymous World
Services, Inc.**
P.O. Box 459
Grand Central Station
New York, NY 10163
(212) 870-3400
alcoholicsanonymous.org

**American Academy of
Addiction Psychiatry**
1010 Vermont Avenue NW,
  Suite 710
Washington, DC 20005
(202) 393 4484
www.painmed.org

**American Academy of Child
and Adolescent Psychiatry**
3615 Wisconsin Ave., NW
Washington, DC 20016
(202) 966-7300
www.aacap.org

**American Anorexia/Bulimia
Association, Inc.**
165 West 46 St., Suite 1108
New York, NY 10036
(212) 575-6200
www.aabainc.org

**American Council for Drug
Education**
164 West 74 Street
New York, NY 10023
(800) 488-DRUG
www.acde.org

**American Foundation For
Suicide Prevention**
120 Wall St. 22nd Fl.
New York, NY 10005
(800) 333-AFSP
www.afsp.org

**American Psychiatric
Association**
1000 Wilson Blvd., Suite 1825
Arlington, VA 22209
(703) 907-7300
www.psych.org

**American Psychological
Association**
750 First Street NE
Washington, DC 20002
(202) 336-5500
www.apa.org

**American Self-Help
Clearinghouse**
Northwest Covenant Medical
  Center
25 Pocono Road
Denville, NJ 07834
(973) 625-3037
www.cmhc.com/selfhelp

**Anxiety Disorders Association
of America**
11900 Parklawn Dr., Suite 100
Rockville, MD 20852
(301) 231-9350
www.adaa.org

**Children and Adults with
Attention Deficit and
Hyperactivity Disorders**
8181 Professional Place,
  Suite 201
Landover, MD 20785
(800) 233-4050
www.chadd.org

**Eating Disorder Referral and
Information Center**
2923 Sandy Pointe, Suite 6
Del Mar, CA 92014
(858) 792 7463
www.edreferral.com

Gamblers Anonymous
International Service Office
P.O. Box 17173
Los Angeles, CA 90017
(213) 386-8789
www.gamblersanonymous.org

Narcotics Anonymous World Services, Inc.
P.O. Box 9999
Van Nuys, CA 91409
(818) 773-9999
www.na.org

National Alliance for the Mentally Ill
200 N. Glebe Road, Suite 1015
Arlington, VA 22203
(800) 950-6264
www.nami.org

National Clearinghouse for Alcohol and Drug Information
P.O. Box 2345
Rockville, MD 20847
(800) 729-6686
www.health.org

National Depressive and Manic-Depressive Association
730 N. Franklin St., Suite 501
Chicago, IL 60610
(800) 826-3632
www.ndmda.org

National Mental Health Association
2001 N. Beauregard Street,
   12th Floor
Alexandria, VA 22311
(800) 969-NMHA
www.nmha.org

Nicotine Anonymous
419 Main Street, PMB#370
Huntington Beach, CA 94159
(415) 750-0328
www.nicotine-anonymous.org

Obsessive Compulsive Foundation
676 State Street
New Haven, CT 06511
(203) 401-2070
www.ocfoundation.org

Overeaters Anonymous
PO Box 44020
Rio Rancho, NM 87174
(505) 891-2664
www.oa.org

Note: There are state and territorial substance abuse agencies that provide information on substance abuse as well as treatment facilities. These are listed in telephone books and online under headings such as Department or Division of Mental Health, Substance Abuse, Addiction, Behavioral Health and Human Services.

BIBLIOGRAPHY & YOUNG ADULT READING LIST

Major sources for facts and statistics in this book, aside from the following texts, were newspapers, journals, magazines, especially *U. S. News & World Report*, *Scientific American*, *National Geographic*, government publications, almanacs, public television specials, documentaries, news broadcasts. Many of the books listed have already been mentioned in the text of this book.

Teen Series Published by Bick Publishing House

Carlson, Dale and Hannah Carlson, M.Ed., C.R.C. *Where's Your Head? Psychology for Teenagers.* 2nd edition. Madison, CT: Bick Publishing House, 1998. A general introduction for adults and young adults to the structure of personality formation, the meaning of intelligence, the mind, feelings, behaviors, biological and cultural agenda, and how to transform our conditioning and ourselves.

___. *Are You Human, or What?* Madison, CT: Bick Publishing House, 2008. Teen guide to the new science of evolutionary psychology, what instincts and behaviors we have inherited from our animal past, what continues to be useful for survival, what we must change in order to survive at all and graduate from human to humane.

___. *Stop the Pain: Teen Meditations.* Madison, CT: Bick Publishing House, 1999. Self knowledge is true meditation: ways to lose the anxiety, hurt, conflict, pain, depression, addictions, loneliness, and to move on.

___. *Who Said What? Philosophy Quotes for Teens.* Madison, CT: Bick Publishing House, 2003. Teen guide to comparing philosophies of the great thinkers of the ages, religious leaders like Jesus and Buddha, philosophers from Socrates to Krishnamurti, scientists like Freud, Einstein, Darwin, Hawking.

___. Edited by Kishore Khairnar, M.A. Physics. *In and Out of Your Mind-Teen Science: Human Bites.* Madison, CT: Bick Publishing House, 2002. Teen guide to all fields of modern science and their ethical use: origin of life and the universe, anthropology and evolution, intellect and intelligence, medical science and genomics.

____. Edited by Nancy Teasdale, B.S. Physics, *The Teen Brain Book: Who and What Are You?* Madison, CT: Bick Publishing House, 2005. Teen guide to understanding the brain, how it works, how you got the way you are, how to rewire yourself, your personality, and what makes you suffer.

____. Foreword by Dialogue Director Kishore Khairnar. *Talk: Teen Art of Communication*, Madison, CT: Bick Publishing House, 2006. Close, powerful relationships are based on communication. How to talk to yourself, to others, to parents, teachers, bosses, sisters, brothers, friends, boyfriends and girlfriends, to groups, to people you don't like, to God.

Carlson, Hannah, M.Ed., C.R.C. *Living with Disabilities*. 2nd edition. Madison, CT: Bick Publishing House, 1997. A 6-volume compendium with sections that describe symptoms, origins, treatments for mental disorders, learning, disabilities, brain defects and injuries. Includes: I Have a Friend with Mental Illness.

____. *The Courage to Lead: Start Your Own Support Group, Mental Illnesses and Addictions*. Madison, CT: Bick Publishing House, 2001.

Krishnamurti, J. *What Are You Doing with Your Life? Books on Living for Teens*. Ojai, California: Krishnamurti Foundation of America, 2001.

____. *Relationships; To Oneself, to Others, to the World, Books on Living for Teens*. Ojai, California: Krishnamurti Foundation of America, 2008.

OTHER SOURCES

Alcoholics Anonymous. *Alcoholics Anonymous* (The Big Book). New York: Alcoholics Anonymous World Services, Inc. 2001.

Al-Anon's Twelve Steps/Twelve Traditions. New York: Alcoholics Anonymous World Services, Inc. 2001.

Beattie, Melody. *Codependent No More*. Center City, MN: Hazelden, 1992.

Cobain, Bev. *When Nothing Matters Anymore: A Survival Guide for Depressed Teens*. Minneapolis, MN: Free Spirit Publishing, 1998.

American Psychiatric Association: *Diagnostic and Statistical Manual of Mental Disorders* (4thEd.) Washington, American Psychiatric Association, 1994.

American Self-Help Clearinghouse. *The Self-Help Sourcebook. Your Guide to Community and Online Support Groups*. Sixth Ed. New Jersey, American Self-Help Clearinghouse, 1998.

C. Roy. *Obsessive-Compulsive Disorder. A Survival Guide for Family and Friends*. New York: Obsessive-Compulsive Anonymous, 1993.

Covey, Sean. *The 7 Habits of Highly Effective Teens*. New York: Simon & Schuster, 1998.

Granet, Roger, MD., Levinson, Robin Karol. *If You Think You Have Depression* (The Dell Guides For Mental Health). New York: Mass Market Paperback, 1998.

Granet, Roger, MD., Ferber, Elizabeth. *Why Am I Up, Why Am I Down?: Understanding Bi-polar Disorder* (The Dell Guides For Mental Health). New York: Mass Market Paperback, 1999.

Gwinnell, Esther, MD, Christine Adamec. *The Encyclopedia of Addictions and Addictive Behaviors*. New York: Facts on File, Inc., 2006.

Hallowell, Edward, M. M.D. Ratey, John J., M.D. *Driven To Distraction: Recognizing and Coping with Attention Deficit Disorder from Childhood Through Adulthood*. New York: Pantheon Books, 1994.

Hoffman, John, and Froemke, Susan, Editors. *Addiction: Why Can't They Just Stop?* New York: Rodale, Inc. and HBO, 2007.

Kaysen, Susanna. *Girl Interrupted*. New York: Vintage Books, 1994.

March, John, S. M.D. *Anxiety Disorder in Children and Adolescents*. New York: Guilford Press, 1995.

Ketchan, Katherine, and Nicholas A. Pace, M.D. *Teens Under the Influence*. New York: Ballentine Books, 2003.

Youngs, Bettie B., Ph.D., Ed.D. and Youngs, Jennifer Leigh. *A Teen's Guide to Living Drug-Free*. Deerfield Beach, FL: Health Communications, Inc. 2003.

INDEX

BICK PUBLISHING HOUSE
PRESENTS
Books for Teenagers

ADDICTION
The Brain Disease
by Dale Carlson and Hannah Carlson, M.Ed., LPC
Pictures by Carol Nicklaus

- What is addiction?
- Addiction to substances
- Addiction to behaviors
- Addiction to the Self
- Treatment and Recovery
- Glossary of Addictions and Meanings

Young adult guide to the physical, emotional, social, psychological disease of addiction. What is addiction? Addiction to substances, behaviors, addictions to ourselves are explored. Self-tests, personal stories, treatment, recovery. Dictionary of addictions.

"Breaks down the stigma regarding the nature of addiction. The raw truth regarding the physical, social, emotional, and psychological aspects of addiction, as well as help and recovery, are presented medically and through personal stories. This book unlocks the door of hope to any suffering from the disease of addiction to substances and/or behaviors. Carlson covers every base from medical neuroscientific information to self-tests to solutions in recovery."

— Jason DeFrancesco, Yale-New Haven Medic

Illustrations, Index, Resources, Self-Screening Tests, Help Telephone Numbers, Websites
114 pages, $14.95, ISBN978-1-884158-35-3

BICK PUBLISHING HOUSE
PRESENTS
A Young Adult Graphic Novel

NEW!

COSMIC CALENDAR:
From the Big Bang to Your Consciousness
by Dale Carlson, edited by Kishore Khairnar, Physicist
Illustrations by Nathalie Lewis

Graphic Teen Guide to modern science relates science to teenager's world.

Our minds, our bodies, our world, our universe—where they came from, how they work, and how desperately we need to understand them to make our own decisions about our own lives.

- Teen guide to modern science
- Physics (no equations except for E-mc2)
- Natural history, physical laws of the universe and our Earth
- Evolution and origin of life, DNA and genomics
- Brain and body, intelligence—human, artificial, cosmic
- Dictionary of science terms
- Websites and links for all sciences
- Teacher's Guide and questions

Cosmic Calendar: Big Bang to Your Consciousness is the Graphic Edition of the award-winning *In and Out of Your Mind: Teen Science, Human Bites*, a New York Public Library Best Books for Teens.

> "Contemplating the connectivity of the universe, atoms, physics, and other scientific wonders…heady stuff. Carlson delves into the mysteries of Earth, and outer and inner space in an approachable way."
>
> — *School Library Journal*

> "Challenges her readers with questions to make them think about the environment, humankind's place in the world, and how ordinary people can help change things for the better."
>
> — *Voice of Youth Advocates*

Graphic Edition of NY Public Library
Best Books for Teens In and Out of
Your Mind: Teen Science
Illustrations, Index, 160 pages, $14.95,
ISBN: 978-1-884158-34-6

BICK PUBLISHING HOUSE
PRESENTS
Books for Teenagers

ARE YOU HUMAN, OR WHAT?
Evolutionary Psychology for Teens

We have evolved from reptile to mammal to human. Can we mutate, evolve into humane?

- Evolution has equipped us, not for happiness, but for survival and reproduction of the species.

- To survive, we are programmed for fear and pain: every one of us had ancestors who managed to survive, mate, and pass on the best adapted programs for staying alive.

- Our brain programs, hardware and software, have already conquered every other species: we've won, we can stop fighting.

- It's time to pay attention to our psychological welfare as well as our technology.

"*Are You Human, or What?* reminds us that we—as nervous, curious people—are not alone. Everyone suffers—and everyone can do something about it."

— *Meghan Ownbey, Teen Editor*

"This book challenges teen/young adult readers to examine their own culturally constructed views while emphasizing that compassion for all, not just 'me and mine' is the only way for each of us to survive."

— *January Welks, Teen Editor*

ForeWord Book of the Year
Illustrations, 224 pages, $14.95, ISBN: 978-1-884158-33-9

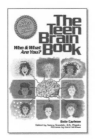

BICK PUBLISHING HOUSE
PRESENTS
Fiction for Young Adults

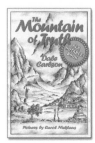

THE MOUNTAIN OF TRUTH
Young Adult Science Fiction
by Dale Carlson
Illustrated by Carol Nicklaus

Teenagers sent to an international summer camp form a secret order to learn disciplines of mind and body so teens can change the world.

"Drugs and sex, both heterosexual and homosexual, are realistically treated…incorporates Eastern philosophy and parapsychology."
— *School Library Journal*

ALA Notable Book
ALA Best Books for Young Adults
224 pages, $14.95, ISBN: 1-884158-30-7

THE HUMAN APES
Young Adult Science Fiction
by Dale Carlson
Illustrated by Carol Nicklaus

Teenagers on an African expedition to study gorillas meet a hidden group of human apes and are invited to give up being human and join their society.

"A stimulating and entertaining story."
— *Publishers Weekly*

ALA Notable Book
Junior Literary Guild Selection
224 pages, $14.95, ISBN: 1-884158-31-5

BICK PUBLISHING HOUSE
PRESENTS

Books for Teenagers
Psychology & Meditation
by Dale Carlson • Hannah Carlson, M.Ed., CRC
NEW EDITIONS

STOP THE PAIN: Teen Meditations
Teens have their own ability for physical and mental meditation to end psychological pain.

- What Is meditation: many ways
- When, where, with whom to meditate
- National directory of resources, centers

"Much good advice...." — *School Library Journal*

New York Public Library Best Book for Teens
Independent Publishers Award
Illustrations, Index, 224 pages, $14.95; ISBN: 1-884158-23-4

WHERE'S YOUR HEAD? Psychology for Teenagers

- Behaviors, feelings, personality formation
- Parents, peers, drugs, sex, violence, discrimination, addictions, depression
- Joys of relationship, friends, skills
- Insight, meditation, therapy

"A practical focus on psychological survival skills."
— *Publishers Weekly*

New York Public Library Books
YA Christopher Award Book
Illustrations, Index, 320 pages, $14.95;
ISBN: 1-884158-19-6

GIRLS ARE EQUAL TOO: The Teenage
Girl's How-to-Survive Book
The female in our society: how to change.

- Girls growing up, in school, with boys
- Sex and relationships
- What to do about men, work, marriage, our culture: the fight for survival.

"Clearly documented approach to cultural sexism."
— *School Library Journal*

ALA Notable Book
Illustrations, Index, 256 pages, $14.95; ISBN: 1-884158-18-8

BICK PUBLISHING HOUSE
PRESENTS
Books on Living for Teens

TEEN RELATIONSHIPS
To Oneself, To Others, To the World
By J. Krishnamurti. Edited by Dale Carlson

- What is relationship?
- To your friends, family, teachers
- In love, sex, marriage
- To work, money, government, society, nature
- Culture, country, the world, God, the universe

J. Krishnamurti spoke to young people all over the world and founded schools in California, England and India. "When one is young." he said, "one must be revolutionary, not merely in revolt...to be psychologically revolutionary means non-acceptance of any pattern."

Illustrations, Index, 288 Pages, $14.95. ISBN: 1-888004-25-8

WHAT ARE YOU DOING WITH YOUR LIFE?
Books on Living for Teenagers
By J. Krishnamurti. Edited by Dale Carlson

Teens learn to understand the self, the purpose of life, work, education, relationships.

The Dalai Lama calls Krishnamurti "one of the greatest thinkers of the age." Time magazine named Krishnamurti, along with Mother Teresa, "one of the five saints of the 20th century."

Translated into five languages.
Illustrations, Index, 288 Pages, $14.95. ISBN: 1-888004-24-X

BICK PUBLISHING HOUSE
PRESENTS

Books for Health & Recovery

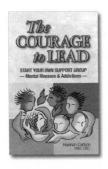

THE COURAGE TO LEAD—Start Your Own Support Group: Mental Illnesses & Addictions
By Hannah Carlson, M.Ed., C.R.C.

Diagnoses, Treatments, Causes of Mental Disorders, Screening tests, Life Stories, Bibliography, National and Local Resources.

"Invaluable supplement to therapy."
— *Midwest Book Review*

Illustrations, Index, 192 pages, $14.95;
ISBN: 1-884158-25-0

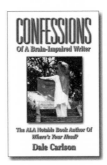

CONFESSIONS OF A BRAIN-IMPAIRED WRITER
A Memoir by Dale Carlson

"Dale Carlson captures with ferocity the dilemmas experienced by people who have learning disabilities...she exposes the most intimate details of her life....Her gift with words demonstrates how people with social disabilities compensate for struggles with relationships."

— Dr. Kathleen C. Laundy, Psy.D., M.S.W.,
Yale School of Medicine

224 pages, $14.95, ISBN: 1-884158-24-2

STOP THE PAIN: Adult Meditations
By Dale Carlson

Discover meditation: you are your own best teacher. How to use meditation to end psychological suffering, depression, anger, past and present hurts, anxiety, loneliness, the daily problems with sex and marriage, relationships, work and money.

"Carlson has drawn together the diverse elements of the mind, the psyche, and the spirit of science...Carlson demystifies meditation using the mirrors of insight and science to reflect what is illusive and beyond words." —
R.E. Mark Lee, Director, Krishnamurti Publications America

Illustrations, 288 pages, $14.95; ISBN: 1-884158-21-8

BICK PUBLISHING HOUSE
PRESENTS

Books on Living
with Disabilities

by Hannah Carlson, M.Ed., CRC • Dale Carlson
Endorsed by Doctors, Rehabilitation Centers, Therapists,
and Providers of Services for People with Disabilities

Living With Disabilities
6-Volume Compendium
ISBN: 1-884158-15-3, $59.70

INCLUDES:
I Have A Friend Who Is Blind
I Have A Friend Who Is Deaf
I Have A Friend With Learning Disabilities
I Have a Friend with Mental Illness
I Have A Friend With Mental Retardation
I Have A Friend In A Wheelchair

"Excellent, informative, accurate."
— Alan Ecker, M.D., Clinical
    Associate Professor at Yale

BICK PUBLISHING HOUSE
PRESENTS

Books on Wildlife Rehabilitation

by Dale Carlson and Irene Ruth
Step-by-Step Guides • Illustrated
Quick Reference for Wildlife Care
For parents, teachers, librarians who want
to learn and teach basic rehabilitation

Wildlife Care For Birds And Mammals
7-Volume Compendium
ISBN: 1-884158-16-1, $59.70

INCLUDES:
I Found A Baby Bird, What Do I Do?
I Found A Baby Duck, What Do I Do?
I Found A Baby Opossum, What Do I Do?
I Found A Baby Rabbit, What Do I Do?
I Found A Baby Raccoon, What Do I Do?
I Found A Baby Squirrel, What Do I Do?
First Aid For Wildlife

First Aid For Wildlife
ISBN: 1-884158-14-5, $9.95
Also available separately.

*Endorsed by Veterinarians, Wildlife Rehabilitation
Centers, and National Wildlife Magazines.*

ORDER FORM

307 NECK ROAD, MADISON, CT 06443
TEL. 203-245-0073 • FAX 203-245-5990
www.bickpubhouse.com

Name: _____

Address: _____

City: _____ State: _____ Zip: _____

Phone: _____ Fax: _____

QTY	BOOK TITLE	PRICE	TOTAL
	TEEN/YOUNG ADULT FICTION		
	The Human Apes	14.95	
	The Mountain of Truth	14.95	
	TEEN/YOUNG ADULT GRAPHIC NONFICTION		
	New! Cosmic Calendar: From the Big Bang to Your Consciousness	14.95	
	TEEN/YOUNG ADULT NONFICTION		
	New! Addiction: The Brain Disease	14.95	
	Are You Human or What?	14.95	
	Girls Are Equal Too: The Teenage Girl's How-To-Survive Book	14.95	
	In and Out of Your Mind: Teen Science: Human Bites	14.95	
	Relationships: To Oneself, To Others, To the World	14.95	
	Stop the Pain: Teen Meditations	14.95	
	Talk: Teen Art of Communication	14.95	
	The Teen Brain Book: Who and What Are You?	14.95	
	What Are You Doing with Your Life?	14.95	
	Where's Your Head?: Psychology for Teenagers	14.95	
	Who Said What? Philosophy Quotes for Teens	14.95	
	ADULT HEALTH, RECOVERY & MEDITATION		
	Confessions of a Brain-Impaired Writer	14.95	
	The Courage to Lead: Mental Illnesses & Addictions	14.95	
	Stop the Pain: Adult Meditations	14.95	
	BOOKS ON LIVING WITH DISABILITIES		
	Living with Disabilities	59.70	
	BOOKS ON WILDLIFE REHABILITATION		
	First Aid for Wildlife	9.95	
	Wildlife Care for Birds and Mammals	59.70	
	TOTAL		
	SHIPPING & HANDLING: $4.00 (1 Book), $6.00 (2), $8.00 (3-10)		
	AMOUNT ENCLOSED		

Send check or money order to Bick Publishing House. Include shipping and handling.
Also Available at your local bookstore from: Amazon.com, AtlasBooks, Baker & Taylor Book Company, Follett Library Resources, and Ingram Book Company.

AUTHOR
Dale Carlson

Author of over 70 books, adult and juvenile, fiction and nonfiction, Carlson has received three ALA Notable Book Awards, the Christopher Award, the *ForeWord* Book of the Year Award, YALSA Nomination Quick Picks for Young Adults, New York Public Library Best Books for Teens, VOYA Honor Book.. She writes science, psychology, dialogue and meditation books for young adults, and general adult nonfiction. Among her titles are *The Mountain of Truth* (ALA Notable Book), *Girls Are Equal Too* (ALA Notable Book), *Where's Your Head?: Psychology for Teenagers* (Christopher Award, New York Public Library Best Books List), *Stop the Pain: Teen Meditations* (New York Public Library Best Books List), *In and Out of Your Mind: Teen Science* (International Book of the Month Club, New York Public Library Best Books List), *Talk: Teen Art of Communication, Wildlife Care for Birds and Mammals, Stop the Pain: Adult Meditations*. Carlson has lived and taught in the Far East: India, Indonesia, China, Japan. She teaches writing here and abroad during part of each year.

CO-AUTHOR
Hannah Carlson, M.Ed., LPC

Past Director of Developmental Disabilities at The Kennedy Center for the Mentally Disabled, at West Haven Community House, Hannah Carlson is author of *Living with Disabilities*, and *The Courage to Lead: Start Your Own Support Group—Mental Illnesses and Addictions*. She is former Senior Therapist and Vocational Counselor/Evaluator at Rusk Institute of Rehabilitation Medicine at New York University Medical Center. She has lectured and taught in her field of the developmentally and traumatically disabled, and is several times published in the international journals "Brain Injury," and in the "Journal of Applied Rehabilitation Counseling." She holds a Masters of Education in Counseling Psychology and a Masters Degree in Developmental Psychology from Columbia University. Carlson is a past Director of the Obsessive Compulsive Foundation, Behavioral Health Specialist for the Connecticut Department of Mental Health and Addictions Services. Currently, she is Senior Director of Dungarvin's Day and Residential Services for Individuals with Developmental Disabilities.

ILLUSTRATOR
Carol Nicklaus

Known as a character illustrator, her work has been featured in *The New York Times*, *Publishers Weekly*, *Good Housekeeping*, and *Mademoiselle*. To date she has done 150 books for Random House, Golden Press, Atheneum, Dutton, Scholastic, and more. She has won awards from ALA, the Christophers, and The American Institute of Graphic Arts.